KU-022-438

This book is dedicated with appreciation to the first teacher who encouraged my talent as a writer, Michael Laurence.

Thank you also to the following people for helping put this book together:

Mark Bego
Dr. William Bradley
Dr. Ruth Burch
Joe Canole
Bill Carter
Dallas Chang
Harry Chapman
Chris Clark
Dr. William Cox
Dana Davidson
Connie Denell
May Dean Eberling
Don Fisher

Mayor Freddie George
John Heidelberg
Venice Johnson
Kathleen Kami
Dick Maurice
Thom McMorris
Anthony Otey
Willard Pugh
Carl Sissac
Daniel Sorine
Vince Waldron
Dr. Jamie Williams
Wesley Wilson

I'd also like to give a special thanks to Bart Andrews and Sherry Robb of the Andrews/Robb Literary Agents. And finally, a warm thank you for their support: Robin Desser and Nancy Coffey.

Oprah!

Robert Waldron

WARNER BOOKS

A *Warner* Book

First published in the United States
by St. Martin's Press in 1987
First published in Great Britain in 1991 by Futura
a Division of Macdonald & Co
Reprinted 1991 (three times)
This edition published by Warner Books in 1992
Reprinted 1993
This updated edition published in 1994

Printed in England by Clays Ltd, St Ives plc

ISBN 0-7515-0086-8

Warner Books
A Division of
Little, Brown and Company (UK)
Brettenham House
Lancaster Place
London WC2E 7EN

A Day with Oprah

"I allow myself to be vulnerable. It's not something I do consciously. But I am. It just happens that way. I'm vulnerable and people say, 'Poor thing. She has big hips too.' "

On a typically cold gray morning in downtown Chicago in March 1985, more than fifty women work their way through the side entrance of the State-Lake Building on West Lake Street. Overhead the rush hour El drowns out their voices as they hurry into the building, not so much to escape the morning chill, but to reach their destination more quickly.

Chicago, as any longtime resident will point out, is a city made up of neighborhoods, and these women attest to the diversity of those neighborhoods. Some live in pink-brick bungalows, complete with a backyard and garage, and wear clothes bought off the rack at stores such as Sears and K Mart. Others reside in lakefront high-rises and purchase their clothes at the fashionable stores along Michigan Avenue.

Bunched together in the crowded elevators, their smiling, anxious faces represent a too-good-to-be-true picture of sisterhood. Blacks, whites, and Hispanics stand together, shoulder to shoulder. You almost expect them to break into a rousing chorus of "I Am Woman." Or, more appropriately, "We Are the World." At this time yesterday, most of them were busy sending their families off to school and work. Today they'll be sharing some of their most intimate sexual experiences with an eager, interested TV viewing public.

The person responsible for making these women feel comfortable enough to broadcast their sex lives publicly is Oprah Winfrey. In January 1984, Oprah had stepped in as host of a locally produced, low-rated TV talk show titled "A.M. Chicago." Previously she had co-hosted "People Are Talking," a popular, locally produced TV talk show based in Baltimore.

Ten years earlier another powerhouse TV talk-show host had made his home in Chicago when he moved his syndicated show from Dayton, Ohio. His name was Phil Donahue and he quickly emerged as Chicago's favorite daytime TV talk-show host, toppling the reigning king and queen of the form, Mike Douglas and Dinah Shore. Whereas Douglas and Dinah succeeded by chatting with such media celebrities as Zsa Zsa Gabor and Pamela Mason, Donahue used his talk show as a forum to confront the hot issues of the day. Controversial topics such as legalized abortion, prostitution, and forced busing were regular fare.

It was an angle David Frost had also employed on his syndicated TV talk show during the early seventies. The wrinkle that set Donahue's show apart from Frost's was that he went into his audience and allowed them to question the show's guests. In an era that brought us the Watergate scandal, Donahue succeeded by involving his audience in the issues presented on his program.

2

Oprah realized that turning "A.M. Chicago's" ratings around would be tough, particularly since she was competing with Donahue, not only in his adopted hometown but in the same time slot. To make matters more difficult, "A.M. Chicago's" issue-oriented format was similar to Donahue's. With the odds clearly in Donahue's favor, a competitive Oprah braced herself for battle.

What Chicago's TV viewing audience didn't anticipate was that Oprah had yet a new wrinkle to add to the talk-show format. By personalizing the issues explored on "A.M. Chicago," it was hoped that Oprah could involve the audience in what she had to offer as a personality.

With Oprah's engaging, unorthodox personality as the drawing card, it didn't take viewers long to turn their attention to "A.M. Chicago." What they found was a host who freely discussed her troubled love life, had problems keeping her weight down, and made no secret of appreciating a good sale. She behaved like the down-to-earth, gregarious next-door neighbor you could trust to spill your deepest, darkest secrets to over a cup of coffee and a slice of pound cake.

For the fifty women boarding the elevators in the State-Lake Building, today was a chance to participate in Oprah's life, as well as share a part of theirs. To become a part of Oprah's studio audience, the women merely had to call a specially designated number, which is usually announced during the show, and request tickets. Often, they know in advance what topic will be explored on the day they plan to visit.

Before being taken to the studio where "A.M. Chicago" is broadcast live, the women are first directed to a smaller studio. An associate producer introduces herself and announces that the guests for today's program are two contributors to a book titled *Our Bodies, Ourselves*. The women are encouraged to jump in with questions they have about their bodies. As they do, each question is written on a large tablet by an associate producer. Next to the question she jots down a quick description of the woman asking it. It's explained that the questions serve as backups in case things run slow.

Meanwhile, down the hall, Oprah is being made up for today's show. Since the show is still local, she doesn't yet have her own personal makeup artist or hairdresser. At this time, though, negotiations are under way for a role in Steven Spielberg's film version of *The Color Purple*, based on Alice Walker's bestseller. *Newsweek* has done a full-page story on Oprah's success in Chicago. She has also appeared on NBC's "The Tonight Show" with Joan Rivers. A deal to syndicate her talk show is on the horizon. But, for now, "A.M. Chicago's" audience is comfortable in believing that Oprah still belongs exclusively to them. It's the same way audiences felt in Baltimore and Nashville when Oprah was still their favored local celebrity.

The dressing room where Oprah is being made up for today's show also serves as the greenroom, a waiting area for the show's guests. One of them stands holding a copy of *Our Bodies, Ourselves*. There's a counter for coffee and popcorn (one of Oprah's favorite snacks), a small table with chairs, and a couch. If an audience member accidentally wandered in she'd probably ask, "This is TV? Where's the glamour?" While the authors chat quietly between themselves, the makeup woman mentions to Oprah that there's a sale going on today at the Midwest Beauty Convention.

With less than thirty minutes before airtime, the audience has been taken to a familiar place, the studio they recognize from their television sets at home. One woman comments to a friend that the set looks so much bigger on her nineteen-inch TV screen. The unspoken question hanging in the air is, "When are we finally going to meet Oprah?"

Outside the studio Oprah can be heard singing "Do Wah Diddy." Unlike "The Tonight Show," there's no Ed McMahon to announce her, nor are there colorful curtains from behind which she will emerge. Instead, Oprah makes her appearance through the same doorway the women walked through twenty minutes earlier. As Oprah greets her audience, they break into a round of spontaneous applause (no, there's no applause sign to cue them). Many of the women smile warmly at Oprah as if they already personally knew her. Standing to the side, a stagehand whispers, "The audience comes to see Oprah more than the guests."

"How many women here today are on the pill?" asks Oprah. Although the women understand that they are expected to jump in, it still feels a little strange to be volunteering such personal information. While a few hands go up tentatively, Oprah admits that she uses birth-control pills. She also confides that she's afraid of facing menopause. "Terrified!" she exclaims. "Does anyone else feel that way?"

As some of the women nod in agreement, others chuckle affirmatively. Out of the corner of her eye Oprah catches sight of an associate producer standing at the doorway holding a small paper bag. As the women talk to each other, Oprah momentarily leaves the studio.

Disappearing to a nearby room, Oprah takes the bag offered by the associate producer. It contains an order of still steaming scrambled eggs. Oprah eats eggs because someone recently told her it would help keep her energy level up during the broadcast. If it works, chances are good she will be passing the tip on to her audience. A few weeks earlier, Oprah had tried taking megadoses of vitamin B-complex, but found herself with so much energy that she felt as if she was bouncing off the walls.

When Oprah returns to the studio, "Good Morning America's" David Hartman and Joan Lunden are seen on the TV monitors bidding their audience farewell. A few years ago Oprah's goal was to succeed Joan Lunden on "Good Morning America." Anchoring five-minute local news segments from Baltimore during "Good Morning America" five mornings a week gave Oprah plenty of time to consider the position and to observe Joan in action. Since arriving in Chicago, however, Oprah's goals have changed considerably. As "Good Morning America" fades out, Oprah waves a pleasant good-bye to David and Joan.

While a commercial wraps, the floor director signals to Oprah with her hand. Holding her microphone, Oprah takes a silent breath and looks into a nearby camera. There's an eerie feeling attached to watching Oprah, or anyone, prepare to greet a television audience live. In less than sixty seconds, the studio audience, now sitting up in their seats sneaking one last glance at themselves on the monitors, will be joined by millions of faceless strangers. You can sense their presence, but because you can't see them, they could just as easily be watching you from a spaceship hovering over Lake Michigan. This almost eerie feeling will surface as a reality the first time a call is taken from a viewer watching at home.

With a cue from her floor director, Oprah greets her home viewing audience with a gracious smile. She's so at ease and warm in her greeting that it is easy to imagine the TV audience sitting less than a foot away from Oprah.

After Oprah introduces the show's guests and explains what the program is about, a woman in the studio audience starts things rolling by asking if the infamous "G" spot really exists. One of the authors answers yes, for some women, and instructs viewers to consult the book for further information. Another woman wants to know if men find it uncomfortable to have sexual intercourse while wearing a rubber. Once again the answer is yes, but only for some men. Viewers are also instructed to consult the book for further information. A caller volunteers that, since having a hysterectomy, she has experienced a tenderness in her breasts. The authors reassure her that this is not unusual and that—to no one's surprise—further information can be found by consulting their book.

With the show in full swing now, women are eagerly raising their hands to ask questions and share observations about their own bodies. Pointing her ever-present microphone at various audience members, Oprah begins to look more like an orchestra leader than a talk-show host.

Although it looks to the audience watching comfortably at home as if Oprah has her attention concentrated completely on her guests and the studio audience, she is, in fact, splitting it in a multitude of different ways. The floor director, with her arms constantly waving at Oprah, looks as if she's taken on the mannerisms of an air-traffic controller. Faster than you can blink an eye, cameras switch back and forth from one to the other. While one camera, its red light beaming, holds on the guests, Oprah huddles with an associate producer in an aisle to quickly exchange notes. Viewed live at the studio. Oprah's show is like watching a videotape run at fast forward. You start wishing for a couple of scrambled eggs yourself.

During a commercial break, Oprah takes time to compliment various audience members on their dress. She also informs the studio audience that she intends to spend her lunch hour today buying discounted makeup at the Midwest Beauty Convention. She suggests they do the same if they're interested in saving money. Oprah makes this announcement with the same kind of naturalness close friends would have exchanging recipes over a backyard fence.

As the show draws to a close, Oprah thanks her guests for making an appearance and also gives their book the expected plug. Even though today's show is now history, the rest of the day will be spent preparing for tomorrow's program.

But first Oprah takes time out to greet each member of her studio audience. This is an important ritual for the audience because it gives them a chance to have personal contact with Oprah. The exchanges have to be brief, however, because studio space is reserved only until eleven o'clock and bumpers, quick spots promoting upcoming shows, still have to be taped.

For most of the women standing in line to greet Oprah it's

enough just to be able to say hello. A few, though, do have requests, usually an autograph or a picture with Oprah. One woman shakes Oprah's hand vigorously and invites her to make an appearance on her family's boat. Another woman dutifully explains that she has been instructed by her mother to extend to Oprah an invitation to visit Mom's beauty salon on the South Side for a complimentary cut.

Later, Oprah confides that these requests aren't unusual. "People want me to come to everything. Barbecues. Picnics. One woman wanted me at her daughter's graduation. Last week a woman said her parents were celebrating their fiftieth anniversary. Could I come to that? Another lady knows I like potatoes and she just wanted me to come over and sit and have a little potatoes and talk!"

This special relationship that Oprah shares with her audience didn't begin in Chicago. Bill Carter, TV critic of *The Baltimore Sun*, who was a guest on "People Are Talking" with Oprah, recalls that "the audience was really enraptured with her. They wanted to touch her. They wanted to reach out to her. They wanted to have some sort of physical contact with her.

"They would remember everything that she ever said," he adds. "They had followed her incredibly closely. They really felt a relationship with her. And she handled them beautifully. She was very patient with them. She chatted with them. She had a lot of respect for them. It was a mutual kind of affection. I was impressed. This was something that was not often seen from someone on television."

"I am those women," says Oprah. "I am every one of them. And they are me. That's why we get along so well.

"White women stop and tell me, 'Everybody says I remind them of you.' And I say, 'But I'm much taller.' It crosses racial barriers.

"I allow myself to be vulnerable. It's not something I do consciously. But I am. It just happens that way. I'm vulnerable and people say, 'Poor thing. She has big hips too.' "

8

Noticing one particularly attractive woman waiting in line, Oprah calls out, "Now I wish I had your legs! Life would be great if I had been born with legs like yours. You're so skinny!" The woman leaves the studio beaming.

With time running short, the floor director gracefully motions for the few remaining women to leave. An associate producer, meanwhile, approaches Oprah to discuss a sensitive topic. The wardrobe mistress needs Oprah's measurements. "Does she have to have them today?" groans Oprah, who is currently on a diet. "Why not in three weeks?"

Kicking off her boots, Oprah takes a seat and begins reading the cue cards. The first card reads, "Tuesday on 'A.M. Chicago,' couples who suffer from impotency." Flubbing the line twice, Oprah releases tension by quipping, "Next week on 'A.M. Chicago,' couples who can't get it up!"

While the crew laughs, Oprah notices the second cue card reads, " 'A.M. Chicago' talks to kids behind bars." "When did this one come up?" asks Oprah.

Receiving an answer from Debbie DiMaio, "A.M. Chicago's" producer, Oprah says, "Who's going to bring them? Or are we going down there? 'Cause I'm sure not gonna bring 'em up here myself!"

As the crew laughs, Debbie suggests Oprah drop the word "talk." Agreeing, Oprah says, "Next week, kids behind bars. We're not gonna talk to them. We're just gonna look at 'em!" If it weren't for the joking, taping the bumpers would be about as interesting for the crew as taping the station's early morning sermonette.

Uncomfortable with the phrasing of another bumper, which invites the audience to use leftover ingredients in their refrigerator for beauty care, Oprah says, "I'm not sure I understand what this means. What are we talking about here? 'You know that old meatloaf in your refrigerator? Put it on your face. Or how about those biscuits from Kentucky Fried Chicken? Use those too!' " Although Oprah is as quick with a quip as any seasoned Las Vegas comedian, she swears she doesn't think of herself as being particularly funny.

Christie Brinkley, who is in Chicago promoting her new line of sportswear, has been booked for the next day's show. Eyeing a cue card that announces her appearance, Oprah says, "Why wasn't I born with a body like hers?" reflecting an attitude no doubt shared by most of her audience.

Someone comments that it has been reported Christie will soon be marrying pop singer Billy Joel. Pondering the kinds of questions she'll ask Christie, Oprah stares off into space and says, "What's it like making love with a short guy? Billy Joel is pretty short, isn't he?" she asks no one in particular.

Before heading back to the combination makeup room/greenroom for a staff meeting to discuss the day's show, Oprah makes time for more pressing business. She has her measurements taken. The dreaded assignation lasts less than five minutes. Walking past the stagehands' room, which is near the wardrobe mistress's room, Oprah calls out, "Now I don't want those measurements leaving this studio!" Turning to an associate producer she adds, "Knowing them, I'll find my measurements written on a flag flying over State Street."

Back in the greenroom, the day's show is reviewed. The consensus is that the guests were too preoccupied with plugging their book. "How many times did they answer a question by saying, 'It's in the book'?" asks Oprah. Reflecting further, she adds, "They were what you call the new feminist woman. Any woman who uses the expression 'support-system' more than once in an hour is definitely into a new way of feminist thinking."

Discussing the audience's participation in the show, everyone agrees that it was best for Oprah to let them carry the program with their questions. "They're really opening up," comments Oprah. "Showing gutsiness. I want them to feel they can ask anything when they're in that studio."

Turning their attention to the next day's show, Christie Brinkley's name is again brought up. It's suggested that Christie's desire to pursue an acting career might be a topic to explore. Reflecting the interests of her audience, Oprah says bluntly, "Who really cares about her acting career? I want to know about her relationship with Billy Joel." Recalling a piece of furniture from Christie's home that stood out in her mind when Barbara Walters interviewed her, Oprah adds, "And where did she get that pink couch shown on her interview with Barbara Walters?"

The possibility that Christie might be a tough interview because of her shyness is mentioned. A staff member fuels this concern by commenting that she'd heard that, for the Barbara Walters interview, they had to shoot three hours of tape to get three good minutes. With Oprah's show broadcast live for sixty minutes, that could spell disaster. As a way of avoiding such a potentially embarrassing situation, another guest has also been booked, a Hollywood makeup artist who has written a book on how to use everyday food products as an alternative to expensive cosmetics. "He's got high energy so we shouldn't have any problem," notes Debbie.

An associate producer suggests that Christie remain to demonstrate makeup techniques with the second guest. At these meetings everyone is encouraged to volunteer ideas. This one, however, is unanimously vetoed.

The following morning Christie arrives with an entourage. Though she looks visibly nervous during the first few minutes of her appearance, she begins to relax as Oprah chats with her about how she met Billy Joel. Nervous gestures, such as running a beautiful hand through her hair and twisting left to right in her chair, fade away. Discussing a song she sang with Billy Joel the

11

night they met she slides comfortably down in her chair, speaking quietly, as if she were at home talking to a close friend.

At the interview's conclusion Christie confesses to an associate producer that she was nervous about appearing on "A.M. Chicago," but adds, "I had a better feeling from that interview than any I've ever done."

Oprah, however, didn't hear Christie's comment until later. She was preoccupied talking with her audience.

1
Oprah's Grandmother

"When my grandmother used to whip my behind, she'd say, 'I'm doing this because I love you.' And I'd want to say, 'If you loved me, you'd get that switch off my butt.' I still don't think that was love."

"We bring you today to Forsyth County, Georgia, just thirty miles north of Atlanta, which in the past few weeks has gained the reputation of being a hotbed of racism," Oprah told her TV viewing audience on February 9, 1987.

Oprah was televising her show live from Cumming, Georgia, to give its residents an opportunity to answer why, in light of the Civil Rights Act, which guarantees blacks the right to live wherever they choose in America, no blacks had been allowed to live in their town since 1912.

Viewers of the network television evening news reports already had etched in their minds an image of what they thought Forsyth County's townspeople looked like. Coverage of two protest marches led by black activists, which had taken place there in January, showed Ku Klux Klan members dressed in white robes yelling, "Go home, nigger!" while young white children waved Confederate flags. Black marchers chanted "We shall overcome," as they ducked to avoid being hit by rocks and bottles hurled at them by angry whites.

"Our sole purpose in coming here," Oprah explained, "is to try and understand the feelings and motivation of all-white Forsyth County. That's what we do every day on this show, explore people's feelings." The decision by Oprah and her staff to include only residents of Forsyth County angered some blacks, causing them to march outside the Dinner Deck restaurant, where the show was being televised. Reverend Hosea Williams, who led the protest, told reporters, "We feel that at best Oprah will project nationwide a false image of the racial problems of Forsyth County. The slogan we are using is, 'Like Forsyth County, Oprah Winfrey has turned all white.' "

What Reverend Williams and his followers failed to understand was that Oprah's decision to include only residents of Forsyth County wasn't made on the basis of race. If Oprah and her staff had included Reverend Williams on the show, she more than likely would have found herself in the midst of a verbal battleground, refereeing a confrontation between Reverend Williams and Frank Shirley, head of the Forsyth County White Patriot Party. By doing things her way, Oprah believed something positive had been accomplished. She told a reporter, "If nothing else, we got the people of the community talking."

Oprah maintains she never experienced racism in her childhood. "It's never been an issue with me," she has said. When asked by a reporter how she'd feel about spending the night in Forsyth County, Oprah responded, "Not very comfortable at all. I'm leaving."

Ironically, Oprah was no stranger to small southern towns. She spent the first six years of her life living in Kosciusko, Mississippi, a rural community pronounced kosy-ESS-ko by its residents. Born on January 29, 1954, she was named Orpah by her Aunt Ida after Ruth's sister-in-law in the Old Testament. A midwife accidentally reversed the letters on her birth certificate. The name Oprah stuck.

Like Forsyth County in the eighties, Kosciusko in the fifties was still basically a segregated community. Unlike Forsyth County, Kosciusko never experienced protest marches, boycotts, or the tensions that America witnessed erupting between blacks and whites in Cumming, Georgia.

"We had a base of what we called good-thinking people, both black and white," recalls Kosciusko's current mayor, Freddie George. "We existed together. We farmed together. We did business with each other."

The willingness of Kosciusko's citizens to treat blacks fairly can be traced to the Polish soldier the town was named after in 1833. Tadeusz Kosciuszko served in George Washington's army during the American Revolution. While stationed in the South, Kosciuszko became acquainted with the injustice of Negro slavery and developed a strong intolerance to it. In his will, he left money to Thomas Jefferson for "the purchase and liberation of Negro slaves." Jefferson referred to Kosciuszko as "the purest son of liberty."

Acknowledging the image most northerners carry of small southern towns, Mayor George says, "If you've never been to Mississippi all you can think about is rednecks and the Ku Klux Klan. That's behind us. Most of it is. I'm not gonna say we still don't have people who are prejudiced. We've got blacks and whites who are prejudiced."

He could have been referring to a situation such as the one brewing in Forsyth County when he added, "An isolated incident sometimes gets blown up in the press. When we get people to our state for any period of time, and they see our people, both black and white, and see how we get along, and how we're making progress here, they are really surprised."

Although now living in Chicago, Oprah harbors no ill will toward Kosciusko. In fact, she still returns occasionally to visit relatives who still reside there, such as her maternal grandparents. "I've read several articles, and I know she's been on several talk shows, and she has mentioned our town," says Mayor George. "Not once has Oprah ever said anything that would show any negativism toward the community. I'm appreciative of that."

Being known as the birthplace of Oprah Winfrey isn't Kosciusko's first brush with fame in the national media. James Meredith, another native of Kosciusko, got national attention during the early sixties when he became the first black to be admitted to the University of Mississippi. The violent resistance by white segregationists to his admission to the university left 160 United States marshals injured, 28 people shot, and 2 men dead. It also made an impression on the people of Kosciusko. "We were just beginning to understand the total scope of the civil rights situation," says Mayor George.

Although Kosciusko isn't exactly as rural or small town as Mayberry, the fictional town depicted in the sixties TV series "The Andy Griffith Show," it does share similarities. Dial telephones weren't installed until 1963. Like Mayberry, Kosciusko's courthouse is in the center of activity, the town square. As is the nature of small-town life, neighbors, at the very least, share a nodding acquaintance with one another.

And passion, if not love, can sometimes be discovered under a large, old oak tree, which is where Oprah was conceived.

The friction that ignited sparks between Oprah's parents, Vernon, twenty, and Vernita Lee, eighteen, came as an unexpected surprise to both of them. Their lovemaking may have been encouraged by the warm evening spring air. By the time winter arrived, Vernon was serving his country as a soldier at an out-of-state base. While some of his military buddies were receiving "Dear John" letters from girlfriends back home, Vernon was surprised to receive from Vernita Lee a "Dear Daddy" letter. Attached to the printed announcement was a note asking him to send clothes.

Many young people Vernita Lee's age found life in a small southern town confining and uneventful, particularly when compared to the fast-paced lifestyle former friends were experiencing in such northern cities as Chicago, St. Louis, and Milwaukee. It didn't help to have job opportunities become more scarce as local businesses, such as Kosciusko's cotton mill, closed. Higher-paying jobs and better living conditions were the promises that lured thousands of blacks during that period to the North. Between the mid-fifties and early seventies, Kosciusko watched as its population declined by almost six thousand. Placing Oprah in the temporary care of her paternal grandmother, Vernita Lee packed her belongings and moved to Milwaukee, where she eventually found work as a cleaning lady.

Oprah doesn't remember much of her mother from her early childhood. Occasionally, Vernita Lee would send for Oprah, determined to begin life as a family for the two of them in Milwaukee, but as a single black mother in the fifties, the obstacles were clearly against her achieving success. By leaving Oprah in her paternal grandmother's care in Kosciusko, Vernita Lee was at least able to give her child a sense of roots and community. Oprah called her grandmother "Momma." They lived on a farm owned by her grandmother. When Oprah was old enough she helped her grandmother tend the farm. Her main chore was to deliver water from a well that was approximately a hundred yards from the house. There was one cow, some chickens, and a few hogs. Oprah's only toy was a corncob doll. Most of the food they ate came from the farm. To this day Oprah isn't sure how her grandmother earned a living. She figures it may have come from selling eggs.

Oprah does remember that she never owned a store-bought dress while living with her grandmother. Her grandmother made all her clothes by hand. If they were poor, Oprah didn't know it. She was clean, well-dressed, and properly fed.

Oprah gives credit to her grandmother for developing her natural talents as a communicator very early. While most three-year-olds are learning to identify colors, Oprah had already been taught to read and write. She was also making Christmas and Easter speeches before packed houses. Today Oprah is often asked to give speeches and is able to command as much as ten thousand dollars per engagement. Her very first speech, delivered at age three, described how Jesus rose on Easter Day. Oprah's clear, concise delivery, free of such awkward and childish mannerisms as fidgeting with her face or hands, caused people to exclaim, "That child is gifted!" The reaction of the Baptist churchgoers on that Easter morning wasn't an isolated incident.

From as early as Oprah can remember, people were always saying, "That child's going somewhere." What has amazed Oprah, looking back on her childhood, is that it all happened. She told Lyn Tornabene of *Woman's Day*, "I don't know why, but somewhere in my spirit, I always knew I was going to be exactly where I am."

At age three, however, Oprah didn't think of herself as being particularly special or gifted. Instead, as she now recalls, she felt lonely, detached, and in constant need of attention. Unfortunately, she didn't always get the love she deserved. She slept with her grandmother in a large feather-bed and remembers being frightened during late-night thunderstorms. At those times her grandmother would place her arms protectively around a terrified, trembling Oprah and gently explain that "God doesn't mess with his children." It is one of the few moments Oprah is able to remember when her grandmother demonstrated physical affection toward her, and this lack of affection would later create problems in Oprah's life.

Early newspaper accounts of Oprah's success as a Chicago TV talk-show host reported that she didn't own her first pair of shoes until she was seven years old. Not true. "I owned them. I just didn't wear them," says Oprah. Her grandmother provided her with two pairs of shoes a year. On Sunday she would go to church wearing patent leather shoes. "I literally didn't wear shoes until Sunday," she says. "I was barefoot all the time because I lived on a farm."

Getting ready for church also meant having her hair braided, a lengthy process that Oprah dreaded. Her grandmother would sit Oprah on her knee, part her hair, and then apply heavy oils to her scalp. It's a procedure that has been practiced on young black girls for generations. The oils made it easier to comb Oprah's hair, but her grandmother mistakenly believed they would also encourage hair growth. After oiling Oprah's hair, her grandmother proceeded to braid it into seventeen plaits. Oprah hated the way her grandmother combed her hair because the style didn't resemble anything remotely close to the ones she observed young white girls in Kosciusko wearing. Instead, their mothers fashioned their curls like Shirley Temple's. Watching the young white girls skip down the street in the town square, Oprah enviously noticed that their hair even bounced.

Today, regular viewers of Oprah's show can see that she now has what she refers to as "bouncin' and behavin'" hair. She learned from her hairdresser, Andre Walker, that the best and simplest way for women, black and white, to have healthy, manageable hair, is simply to rotate their regular brand of shampoo and conditioner with different brands on a daily basis. Oprah once informed her audience that there were still blacks who heavily greased their scalps "and wonder why their hair doesn't move. The reason it doesn't move is because there's too much stuff in it. It's quite possible to have black hair, and not oil it, and have that hair be strong hair." If Oprah's grandmother had known this in the fifties, it quite possibly could have prevented Oprah, like many other young black girls, from envying white girls because of their hair.

The nearest neighbor to Oprah's grandmother was a blind man who lived up the road. The only friend Oprah had who was anywhere near her own age was a girl named Glenda Ray, who lived down the road in an impressive brick house. Oprah eagerly looked forward to those days when she could visit Glenda Ray, not only because of the companionship she provided, but also because Glenda Ray's mother, who was a schoolteacher, bestowed upon her daughter an ample supply of toys and, best of all, real dolls, not ones made out of corncob. These were dolls whose hair you could comb. If you wanted, you could even feed them with a bottle, or lull them quietly to sleep. Oprah would spend hours mothering her friend's dolls.

Unfortunately, the visits to Glenda Ray's house were few and far between. One morning, determined to spend time at Glenda Ray's, Oprah attempted to walk there alone. When Oprah's grandmother located her, she gave Oprah a beating.

Hungry to connect with others, Oprah befriended her grandmother's farm animals, even giving them names. The animals were a receptive audience to Oprah, who rehearsed her church speeches for them. It's amusing and touching to consider that Oprah's audience today, which is numbered in the millions nationwide, started with a cow, some chickens, and a few hogs.

When company would arrive to visit her grandmother, an affectionate Oprah's first inclination would be to shower them with kisses and hugs. Neighbors found Oprah extremely likable because she was always eager and able to hold a lively conversation with them. Oprah's grandmother, however, belonged to a generation that firmly believed children should be seen and not heard. Rather than allow Oprah to visit with the grown-ups, she would order the little girl to sit in a corner and keep quiet. And though her grandmother thus excluded her, Oprah was at the same time grateful to her grandmother for teaching her the joys of reading and writing. Besides helping her to pass the time, reading introduced her to new worlds. Still, Oprah couldn't resist observing and listening to conversations her grandmother would have with company. This often got her into trouble.

"Cousin Molly, who lived up the road, used to come and visit all the time," recalls Oprah. But Cousin Molly had an annoying habit. "She'd pick her nose," Oprah says. "I used to sit there and imitate her picking her nose." Catching Oprah mirroring Cousin Molly's bad habit angered Oprah's grandmother, causing her to physically discipline Oprah.

Oprah boasts that she was quite adept at performing very accurate imitations of her grandmother's friends. "Whoever would come to visit my grandmother, I'd go in the back room and I'd be imitating them. I'd do all their voices." Rather than recognize Oprah's natural dramatic talent, her grandmother chose to view it as insolence. She believed the only way to correct Oprah's behavior was by whipping her. Unlike other children who learned from their mistakes and would avoid repeating them to keep from being whipped again, Oprah brashly made no attempt to alter her behavior.

"I was always getting into trouble and I always thought I could get away with it," she told Lyn Tornabene of *Woman's Day*. "You couldn't just say 'I won't do it anymore.' The other thing is, in the middle of the whippings they'd say, 'now shut up, now shut up,' and you couldn't even cry." Sometimes Oprah's beatings were so severe that large welts would develop on her back.

"Those were the days when people whipped you because they could," said Oprah. "You got a whipping just because you got on somebody's nerves. Whereas today

21

your child will report you and that will be called child abuse."

Although Oprah readily acknowledges today that her grandmother was guilty of child abuse, she says that as a child she was defenseless against doing anything to stop it. How could she? Neighbors didn't recognize the signs of child abuse. There weren't TV talk shows shedding light on the subject to educate people. Women's magazines were more concerned with presenting recipes than enlightening their readers about important, necessary topics. Indeed, in the fifties beating a child wasn't even considered child abuse; it was called disciplining. As a result, her grandmother's brand of punishment, particularly in the South, was considered socially acceptable behavior. Even today there are parents who wouldn't think twice about taking a strap to their children and beating them until they left bruises.

Recalling the whippings she received on a regular basis, Oprah says, "If I didn't get one that day it would be saved up until Saturday because Saturday was bath-bathing time.

"I remember one day I had gotten a mighty whipping. I had gone to the well to get some water. And I was singing to myself, as I always did. Singing 'Zippity Do-dah,' walking through the pasture, dipping my fingers into the water, just a-playing with it and splashing it all over. I did not know my grandmother had intended this to be drinking water. So I got to the house and she says, 'Girl, were you playing in that water?' I said, 'No, ma'am,' with water dripping all over my hands. She said, 'I'm gonna get you for that.' I didn't get a whipping for three days. Three days passed and I thought, 'Well, she forgot that whipping.' "

Saturday arrived and Oprah still hadn't received a whipping for the incident. Bath-bathing took place on Saturday, and because there wasn't indoor plumbing at

Oprah's grandmother's house, it was an event. To get the water needed for their baths Oprah would have to carry endless pails of water from the well. "You'd heat the water in the tin tubs and all that stuff." Finished with her bath on that particular Saturday, Oprah stood up to step out of the tin tub and was " 'naked as a jaybird,' as my grandmother used to say."

Standing before a naked, shivering Oprah was her grandmother. To Oprah's horror her grandmother wasn't holding a towel out to dry her off. Instead, she had a switch in her hands. Looking at Oprah she said, "Do you remember last Tuesday?"

Oprah knew from past experience that a whipping received right after a bath was the worst of all because the warm water relaxed the nerve endings, drawing them closer to the surface. In a futile attempt to keep her grandmother from whipping her, Oprah pleaded, "No, Momma, no!" She even tried tears. "I could cry on cue." But this time even tears didn't deter her grandmother from giving her the whipping she felt Oprah deserved.

Another time, Oprah recalls, "I was out in the smokehouse. You know, where they kept hams, rice, and stuff like that. I accidentally knocked one down one day and spilled a whole barrel of rice." Oprah remembers the fear she felt that day looking at "rice all over the floor." When her grandmother saw what Oprah had done she immediately whipped her. A young Oprah couldn't understand why her grandmother had whipped her because "it was an accident."

"I was washing dishes, broke a glass, and got a whipping for that."

Finally, Oprah one day threatened to run away. Standing up to her grandmother she cried, "You're not gonna whip me another day!" Remembering the incident she now says, "I paid for that one."

When it came time for a whipping, her grandmother

23

would sometimes send Oprah outside to choose the weapon that would be used against her. She told Lyn Tornabene of *Woman's Day*, "You go and pull a little limb off a tree and you bring it in. It's what Richard Pryor described as the longest walk in your life—to get your own switch." When Oprah's grandmother thought the indiscretion deserved it, she would braid three switches together, "just in case one wore out."

Obviously, Oprah's childhood experiences with her grandmother inform her current opinions about bringing up children. On a show discussing corporal punishment in schools, Oprah became alarmed when a guest advocated the practice in inner-city schools because he believed it showed the children you cared about them.

"Our prisons are filled with older men who, as young men, had the living hell beat out of them," Oprah said. "Every parent who beat them said, 'I'm doing this because I love you.' When my grandmother used to whip my behind, she'd say, 'I'm doing this because I love you.' And I'd want to say, 'If you loved me, you'd get that switch off my butt.' I still don't think that was love."

Looking back on her early childhood and the punishment her grandmother frequently doled out, Oprah told me, "I certainly do think that many of the whippings I received were unnecessary. I believed it at the time and"— she paused and looked toward the ceiling as she called out—"I believe it today, Grandmomma! Let me tell you!"

On a show examining the effects of verbal abuse on children, Oprah took a call from a distraught viewer who confided she was upset because she had spanked her three-year-old. Later, a black woman in the studio audience stood up and discussed the whippings she had received as a child. Oprah commented to her audience, "I really do think there's a difference just with my white friends growing up and my black friends growing up." Referring to the caller she added, "This woman is feeling traumatized because she spanked her three-year-old, when, as black children, we had a whipping every day of our lives. That's sort of like what you went through."

Although Oprah knew how to read and write by age three, other children her age had already viewed their first full-length color movie, usually one produced by Walt Disney, such as *Dumbo* or *Cinderella*. Oprah considered herself lucky just to be able to catch a glimpse of television. This treat would occur maybe once or twice a year when visiting friends or family on holidays. What impressed Oprah watching television was how white children, such as Beaver Cleaver, seemed privileged. They lived in huge, expansive homes with yards that had neatly trimmed lawns. More important, they didn't get whippings. The last thing Oprah could imagine was June or Ward Cleaver taking a strap to Beaver. She marveled at how Beaver could get away with the very things she couldn't. When Beaver tried to run away he didn't receive one single, solitary lick from Ward. Instead, good old Ward sat Beaver down, and in a patient, loving manner, tried to help Beaver understand the error of his ways. What Oprah didn't realize as a child was that there were also a lot of white kids watching "Leave It to Beaver" who also wondered how he got off so lucky. Oprah has asked herself, "What would've happened if I had had the kind of grandmother who, instead of beating my butt, would've sat me down to discuss, you know, my feelings over the matter?"

Adopting a kindly, grandmotherly voice, Oprah imitated what her grandmother would have sounded like as she tried to be understanding, "Now, tell me, little girl, why were you playing in the water on the way from the well?"

Reflecting on how such an unlikely scenario would have altered the course of her life, Oprah said, "Perhaps I could've been more sensitive."

"It's interesting how people have different ways of showing love," Oprah once said on her show. "So many of us grow up with June Cleaver in our mind. We think that's the way it is. So, as a child, if your mother doesn't have milk and cookies waiting for you when you get home, you think that everybody else's mother is doing that and they're packing nice little lunches with love and saying, 'Go off and have a great day, Suzie!' When that doesn't happen you feel traumatized in many ways."

Oprah revealed to a journalist that as a child she went to bed at night praying for Shirley Temple curls like the white girls had. She'd close her eyes at night hoping that when she woke up in the morning she'd be white. As a way of helping the process along, Oprah slept with two cotton balls on her nose, snapped together by a wooden clothespin. She thought this would get her nose to turn up rather than grow out flat. The clothespin was so cumbersome that she had difficulty breathing. When she'd wake up in the morning, all she'd find were two clothespin prints on the side of her nose. But the main reason she wanted to be white was because white children, such as Beaver Cleaver, didn't get whippings.

Nonetheless, Oprah retains a deep love for her grandmother. "You know, I am what I am today because of my grandmother: my strength, my sense of reasoning, everything, all of that, was set by the time I was six years old. I basically am no different now from what I was when I was six years old."

On a holiday show featuring American heroes, one of Oprah's guests was a man named Bob Wieland, a veteran who, despite the loss of both legs in the Vietnam War, had recently completed a 2,784-mile Walk for Hunger across America. He told Oprah, "It's literally impossible to stop a man or woman from achieving what it is they want to achieve. It took me 4,900,016 steps to get across America. You know what step was the most difficult? The first one.

But once that first step was taken it turned out to be the easiest 'cause that was one step closer to the goal." The audience's hush was a token of their deep respect for this man's strength and courage.

"Weren't there some steps in the middle that were pretty hard?" Oprah asked, good-naturedly, and then, to make her audience relax and laugh, she said, "I mean, really, Bob! Right around Kansas? Goin' through all that hay . . . Gettin' all that hay stuck between your fingers. Wasn't that pretty hard?" The studio audience let out a collective sigh and giggled.

As a toddler Oprah took her first tiny steps on her grandmother's farm. When she was six years old, her mother, Vernita Lee, returned to take Oprah back with her permanently to Milwaukee. For Oprah, the journey from her grandmother's dilapidated farm in Kosciusko, Mississippi, to urban Milwaukee would represent the first major steps she would take to get her where she is today.

2
Oprah and Her Mother

"My mother was the best-dressed maid ever known to woman. You know how you see women going to work at the nice white people's houses wearing slacks? My mother would put on high-heel shoes and her suede skirt and go steppin'."

After six years of living in Milwaukee, Oprah's mother had made quite a few changes in her life. The most significant was the birth of another child, also a girl. Unlike Oprah, Vernita Lee's second daughter was light-skinned. Since this was the early sixties, when blacks were still called Negroes and being black wasn't necessarily equated with being beautiful, there were still blacks who considered it a coup to be born light-skinned; the standard of beauty was determined by the fairness of one's skin. A comparison in white culture would be the premium some of us place on being born blond and blue-eyed.

Oprah recalls that her light-skinned half sister was showered with attention. She believes this happened because her half sister was the prettiest. Oprah was considered the smart one, but in her eyes that didn't count for much. She never received praise for being smart. Instead, people teased her because she was always sitting in a corner reading. It made Oprah feel sad and left out. She turned to books for companionship.

Oprah couldn't understand why Vernita Lee had wanted them to live together as a family in Milwaukee. It wasn't as if they had a home of their own. Instead, Vernita Lee rented one room for all three of them in a house owned by a close friend. It was clear to Oprah that her mother wasn't prepared to feed another mouth. She felt like an outcast and feared she was nothing more than an extra burden on Vernita Lee.

Attending school didn't help to make Oprah feel any less of an outsider. While the other students struggled to master the alphabet, Oprah, already skilled at reading and writing, was way beyond them. Considered a bookworm and teacher's pet by her classmates, it came as no surprise to them when Oprah received outstanding grades. Impressed by Oprah's brightness, her first-grade teacher decided to have her skip a grade.

Despite their poor, cramped living conditions, Vernita Lee set a goal to see that her children were well-dressed and clean. She felt that just because they were poor they didn't have to look it. Even during their bleakest periods, when Vernita Lee was forced to apply for welfare, she managed to keep up appearances, for herself and her children.

Oprah recalls that when her mother was working as a maid she never left the house wearing her uniform. "My mother was the best-dressed maid ever known to woman," she says. "You know how you see women going to work at the nice white people's houses wearing slacks? My mother would put on high-heel shoes and her suede skirt and go steppin'." Seeing Vernita Lee, a lone black face on an otherwise all-white bus, the other passengers couldn't determine what she did for a living. "It was very important for her not to look the part," says Oprah. "She'd get her hair done and go to work."

Like most children, Oprah longed to have a pet. She pleaded with Vernita Lee to let her have a dog, but her mother said it was out of the question. She could barely afford to feed them. Where would she find the money to feed a dog too?

An ever-industrious Oprah soon found what she considered a workable solution to her dilemma. The house they lived in was swarming with roaches, and no one did anything to get rid of them. "Now I know roaches are supposed to be such a horrible thing," she told an *Ebony* journalist, "Well, hell, we had hundreds of them. It didn't occur to me they were so bad." What would be so wrong with making pets out of the roaches? reasoned Oprah.

Retrieving a discarded mayonnaise jar from the trash, Oprah punched holes in its lid. The jar would serve as a home for her new pets. After all, that's what kids put lightning bugs in when they caught them. "You can't catch lightning bugs in the wintertime, so I'd keep roaches in a jar," Oprah was quoted in *Interview* magazine. "I would name them and put them in a jar and feed them . . . like kids catching lightning bugs." She recalled that she named two of the roaches Melinda and Sandy. To Oprah's dismay, her pet roaches have received almost as much attention in the media as her Oscar nomination for her performance in *The Color Purple*. "I'm so sick of hearing about those damn roaches!" she says.

Despite her best efforts, Vernita Lee found herself feeling insecure as a provider for her daughters. She wanted them to have the best, but as a single black parent there were terrible obstacles for her to overcome. Aware of the difficulties Vernita Lee was facing, Oprah's father, Vernon, now living in Nashville, asked Vernita Lee if Oprah could come and live with him and his wife, Zelma. Zelma's recent miscarriage had left the couple childless, and though they considered trying again, they feared the risks Zelma might encounter if she were to become pregnant again. Having Vernon's child, Oprah, come to live with them seemed like a logical alternative.

Vernon had relocated to Nashville after leaving the army in 1955. He quickly found two jobs, one as a janitor at Vanderbilt University and the other as a pot washer at City Hospital, which paid only seventy-five cents an hour. He called his work as a pot washer the "worst job in Nashville."

Realizing that Vernon and Zelma could provide a more financially stable environment for Oprah, Vernita Lee reluctantly consented. The move didn't seem to create a problem for Oprah, and she left the Milwaukee house to join her father in Nashville.

Life with father and stepmother provided some stiff challenges for Oprah. Quizzing her new daughter on her studies, Zelma discovered the eight-year-old hadn't yet learned how to multiply, something she would need to know as she began third grade in a Nashville school. Wanting Oprah to be fully prepared, Zelma spent the entire summer drilling her stepdaughter on the multiplication table. Once school began she also had Oprah supplement her regular school studies with ancillary assignments to be completed at home. Besides reading a book a week and writing a report on it, Oprah was also required to increase her vocabulary by a set number of words per week.

Unaccustomed to the firm guidelines she was expected to follow in her father's home, Oprah felt as if she were living at a military school. Still, she understood that the boundaries set by her father and stepmother were based on love. Oprah surprised even herself when at school she found herself becoming more outgoing—and more popular with her peers than she'd ever been before.

One of Oprah's fondest memories from that first year spent with her father and stepmother were the career goals she set for herself. "I wanted to be a missionary for the longest time!" Her goal came close to being realized as a third-grader. "I was a missionary for Costa Rica, let me tell you. I used to collect money on the playground every single day of the year. I was a maniac."

Religion suddenly took on a deep significance. Since Zelma and Vernon were active members of Faith United Church, Sundays were spent in the house of God. Touched by the lively and emotional sermons delivered by Faith United's minister, Oprah even considered becoming a preacher when she grew up. Her third-grade teacher often turned the floor over to Oprah, recognizing her gifts as a communicator. "On Monday mornings I led devotion in class, with graham crackers and milk," Oprah reminisces. Standing before the class, Oprah would also convey the importance of helping out the starving kids in Costa Rica. She would paint vivid pictures through her amazing gift for language of the suffering there, persuading her classmates to contribute their nickels and dimes during recess. On Sundays Oprah would turn the money she collected over to the missionary fund.

Meanwhile in Milwaukee, Vernita Lee was beginning to have second thoughts about having given up her eldest daughter. Yanking Oprah out of school in the middle of the year would have been too unsettling, she knew, but she made arrangements with Vernon to let Oprah spend the summer with her. And from the moment Oprah returned to Milwaukee, her mother began pressuring her little girl to stay. Vernita Lee sensed that Oprah enjoyed the security her father's marriage offered, and she quickly informed Oprah that she planned to marry, too. Vernita had had another baby since Oprah had last seen her, and Oprah learned the man Vernita Lee intended to marry was a boyfriend her mother had been seeing regularly for years, the father of this third child, a boy. With Vernita Lee's promise that they'd become an honest-to-goodness, genuine family, Oprah agreed to stay. Such decisions are, of course, enormously difficult, especially for a child as young as Oprah was at that time.

When Vernon arrived at the end of summer to take Oprah back to Nashville, he immediately knew something was wrong. Seeing Oprah, he barely recognized the spirit she had possessed living in his home. She was quiet and withdrawn, barely able to muster up a simple hello to him.

That's when Vernita Lee dropped her bombshell. She announced she had had a change of heart about letting Oprah return to Nashville. Instead, she wanted Oprah to remain with her. Since Vernon hadn't secured legal custody of Oprah, there was nothing he could do to alter the situation. He returned to Nashville without Oprah. It was the only time in his life he had ever cried over his daughter, Vernon confessed to a *Washington Post* reporter. "We had brought her out of that atmosphere, out of a house into a home, so I knew it was not good for her, being in that environment again."

Living with Vernita Lee again, Oprah was no longer required to read a book a week and report on it. The live-in father she had been told she would acquire never materialized. A disappointed Oprah once again sought escape in books. She also began spending her hours after school watching television. Her favorite programs were "Leave It to Beaver," "I Love Lucy," and "The Andy Griffith Show."

Watching television inspired her. The first time she saw Diana Ross perform with the Supremes on "The Ed Sullivan Show" made quite an impact. She couldn't recall ever having seen black women, glamorously dressed, singing on TV. Suddenly, the possibilities of what she could become in life seemed limitless.

It was also while watching television that Oprah learned about the assassinations of President John Kennedy, Dr. Martin Luther King, Jr., and Senator Robert Kennedy. Her mother's tearful reaction to Dr. King's death was, "Oh, Lord!

Oh, Lord! They shot him!" All of the assassinations left Oprah, like most Americans, feeling devastated.

When Oprah returned to Milwaukee her continued good grades served as an irritant to some of her classmates. Her unwillingness to become involved in violent schoolyard confrontations left her branded as a chicken. Her skills as a communicator combined with her knowledge of the Bible saved Oprah from one potentially ugly schoolyard incident. She recalls that, one day, "these kids were gonna gang up and beat my butt. There were six of them." Unwilling to trade punches with them, Oprah fell back on a Bible story. "I had just read the story of Jesus of Nazareth coming into the city, laying palms on the ground to the people, and how all these people were pissed at him." Oprah told the story to the six bullies, reminding them that people had thrown stones at Jesus. She spoke clearly and calmly to the gang. "In spite of that, he had love in his heart for them. And though you are throwing stones at me, I am going to try and love you and forgive you and maybe then you can still get into Heaven." Oprah's story had the desired effect. "They didn't beat me up," she says today, laughing.

Probably the most traumatic incident Oprah had to overcome growing up took place when she was nine years old. One evening she was left at a relative's house, in the temporary care of a nineteen-year-old male cousin, who was a frequent babysitter to Oprah. Oprah didn't feel comfortable around her cousin; she instinctively suspected the interest he took in her. There was one bed in the apartment Oprah had been taken to and she was expected to share it with him. That night, he raped her.

The following morning her cousin took Oprah to the zoo. As a bribe to keep her quiet, he bought her an ice cream cone. The bribe was unnecessary. Oprah had no intention of revealing to anyone what had happened between them. Although she didn't fully understand what had occurred, Oprah knew it was wrong. What she didn't realize was that she wasn't responsible. Oprah believed if she told someone what had taken place, the finger of blame somehow would have been directed at her.

The following fall Oprah was introduced to the facts of life on the school playground. A classmate graphically explained to a horrified Oprah how babies were made. Oprah immediately feared she had become pregnant. "Every time I had a stomachache," she told *People* magazine, "I thought I was pregnant and asked to go to the bathroom so if I had it nobody could see.

"That for me was the terror: Was I going to have it, how would I hide it, all the people would be mad at me, how could I keep it in my room without my mother knowing?"

Although her cousin never attempted sexual molestation again, there were other men, friends of the family, most notably a boyfriend of Vernita Lee's, who sexually abused Oprah. That it happened again, repeatedly, with other men only reinforced Oprah's mistaken belief that she was responsible. She told *USA Today*, "I know what it is like to lie in bed and know that other person is there, and you are pretending you are asleep, hoping he won't touch you."

It didn't occur to Oprah that she had been sexually abused until years later, when she was in Baltimore, interviewing a victim of sexual abuse. The woman's story struck a familiar chord. For the first time, Oprah understood what had happened to her. What surprised Oprah was that it had happened to other people, too.

Still, it wasn't until Oprah began hosting "A.M. Chicago" that she was finally able to discuss openly her history of being sexually abused. The topic of the show was incest. After listening to a middle-aged woman painfully recount to the audience the circumstances behind her autistic son's birth, that he was also her father's child, Oprah broke down and wept. Embracing the woman, Oprah explained that she had also been the victim of sexual abuse. She hadn't expected to be so candid with her audience. The admission was made impulsively, during an emotional moment. Immediately after the show, Oprah's staff received close to a thousand calls from people who said, "It happened to me, what can I do?"

Oprah once said, "My biggest fault is that I do not express anger very well." Remarkably, she doesn't feel anger toward her abusers. By the same token, she hasn't forgiven them, either. Acknowledging the validity of the rage women feel for their abusers, Oprah nevertheless confesses that, for her, the emotion would have become too consuming. "What I've learned about being angry with people is that it generally hurts you more than it hurts them. All the anger that you're trying to vent breeds so much frustration."

Rather than going through life saying, "I'm this way because I was sexually abused as a child," Oprah believes a more positive approach is to accept the responsibility not for what happened but for *overcoming* what happened to her. "I understand that there are a lot of sick people in the world," she says. "I understand that many people are victimized, and some people certainly more horribly than I have been. But you have to be responsible for claiming your own victories, you really do. If you live in the past and allow the past to define who you are then you never grow."

Approaching adolescence while living in Milwaukee with her mother presented a new set of challenges for Oprah, particularly when it came to boys. "I was 36-23-36 at age thirteen, which created a few problems. I was not allowed to talk to boys. And they were everywhere!"

Discussing single-parent families on her show, Oprah said, "This happens in a lot of families where there's a single parent and the mother runs the family: there are boyfriends going in and out of the house and daughters, particularly, see this. Mothers say, 'Don't let some man do this. You keep your dress down! You do what I say!' When what the child sees is entirely different from what the mother is saying.

"I had that when I was a kid. 'Do as I say, not what I do.' But that doesn't work. Doesn't work."

At thirteen Oprah also entered high school. She attended Lincoln High School, situated in a poor section of Milwaukee near her home. A teacher immediately discerned that Oprah was different from Lincoln's typical student. For the most part, Lincoln's student body was rowdy and apathetic about the education they received. Oprah, on the other hand, was well-mannered, bright, and eager to learn. She would spend her lunch hour sitting quietly in a corner reading, while other students were throwing spitballs in the lunchroom. Realizing that Oprah's potential was being wasted at Lincoln, the teacher arranged a full scholarship for her at a private, affluent high school called Nicolet, which was twenty miles from her home. Oprah recalls that she felt like "the only Negro child walking those halls."

Not that Oprah felt ostracized because she was black, quite the contrary. It was 1968. Blacks were demanding their rights more aggressively than ever before in American history. Dr. King's nonviolent approach to civil rights was being challenged by emerging black activist leaders who advocated violence as a way of obtaining equal rights for blacks. With the ensuing riots that followed Dr. King's assassination, whites developed a different attitude toward blacks. This was very apparent to Oprah while she was attending Nicolet. "I was the most popular thing there," she says. "People were very cautious about blacks."

Her classmates called her Opey. Learning that their children were taking classes with a "Negro girl," mothers would enthusiastically encourage their children to invite Oprah home with them after school. "Like I was a toy," observes Oprah.

As soon as Oprah would arrive at these white, upper-middle-class homes, Pearl Bailey records would begin spinning on the turntable, Oprah wryly recalls. The maid would be yanked out of the kitchen to talk to her. The parents assumed that, because they were both black, they already knew each other and would have lots to talk about. Neighbors would suddenly materialize and Oprah would be introduced as the "Negro friend." Conversations would revolve around black sports figures and entertainers. "They'd all sit around talking about Sammy Davis, Jr., like I knew him," says Oprah.

Suffering through the ignorance of isolated, well-intentioned whites, as they sat comfortably in their wall-to-wall-carpeted, dishwasher-equipped, two-story homes, was a breeze compared to the dread Oprah faced night after night as she returned to her own cramped, two-bedroom apartment. She soon realized she was receiving an education from Nicolet she hadn't bargained for. As her world expanded the perceptions of the neighborhood she called home were being dramatically altered. "For the first time I understood that there was another side. All of a sudden, the ghetto didn't look so good anymore."

It was—and perhaps still is—a unique and rare event for a thirteen-year-old black girl from a lower-class neighborhood to venture into an upper-class, all-white neighborhood, and witness firsthand the insides of the homes in that neighborhood. It's one thing to watch shows such as "Dynasty" or "Dallas" on television and fantasize about being wealthy. It's quite another to see with your own eyes that not only are there people who live better than you, but that these people are your fellow classmates, kids you sit next to in school—and, incidentally, kids you receive better grades than. You can't help but wonder, why don't I live like that? Usually, what follows is, what's wrong with me that I can't live like that?

"I used to take three buses to get back home twenty miles every day," Oprah recalls. Imagine you were taking that bus ride back home. Riding those twenty miles you'd notice you were leaving a neighborhood where the houses are beautiful and spacious, with lush, green lawns, for a neighborhood where the buildings are old and rundown, with cracked sidewalks that are littered with broken glass and debris. How would it affect you knowing you had to live in this neighborhood? Then ask yourself, how would it affect a bright, yet troubled and confused, thirteen-year-old girl? "It was like going back to Cinderella's house from the castle every night," Oprah says.

Riding the bus through the suburbs, the only other blacks Oprah encountered were women who worked as maids, just like her mother. Oprah says she felt angered that her mother had to work as a maid, but adds, "I adjusted to it. It's really no big deal. It is no big deal. I think people become what they can in life. You do what you can."

Because Vernita Lee struggled to make ends meet, there wasn't extra money available for Oprah to do the things her new, wealthier friends could effortlessly afford thanks to the generous allowances they received from their parents. When they would invite Oprah to join them for a pizza and a shake, Oprah felt pressured. In an attempt to keep up with her new friends, Oprah started stealing money from Vernita Lee's purse.

As her adolescent daughter struggled with her changing identity, Vernita Lee found herself coping with problems she doubted she was equipped to handle. Oprah began to want not just money for pizza or new clothes, but a father at home. "I wanted a normal family," she says. "I wanted a family like everybody else because I was going to a school where kids had mothers and fathers. I used to make up stories about my mother and my dad. I told the biggest lies about them because I wanted to be like everybody else."

Oprah's discontent began to spread beyond her home

and her family. She became unhappy with herself. Looking in the mirror, all she could see was an ugly poor girl. Even the butterfly frame glasses she wore mocked her. She considered them unstylish, like something an oldmaid librarian would wear. Oprah asked her mother for a pair of hipper, octagonal glasses, like the other kids wore. But Vernita Lee responded that she couldn't afford them.

Obsessed with owning new glasses, Oprah hatched a plan. "I staged a robbery, broke my glasses, and pretended to have amnesia," she later told Joan Rivers. "I stayed home from school one day and stomped the glasses on the floor into a million pieces. I pulled down the curtains. I knocked over the lamps. I called the police. I laid myself on the floor."

Oprah was rushed to the hospital, where she explained to the doctors she was suffering from amnesia. When the police managed to locate Vernita Lee, they drove her to the hospital to see her daughter. Vernita was shaken, until she learned from the police that the only thing damaged in the burglary was Oprah's eyeglasses.

Not long after Oprah returned home, trouble resurfaced in the guise of a young puppy. After years of unrelenting requests from her children for a dog, Vernita Lee finally consented to letting them have one. Unfortunately, the children had a hard time housebreaking the puppy. After spending all day cleaning other people's houses, the last thing Vernita Lee wanted to see when she came into her own living room was a mess made by a puppy with a bladder problem. She announced that the puppy had to go.

Determined to keep it, Oprah concocted a complicated scheme designed to make it look as if the puppy had thwarted a robbery attempt. To complete the scenario, Oprah tossed her mother's jewelry out a bedroom window. Of course, when Vernita Lee discovered what had taken place, she was furious.

Things finally came to a head when Oprah decided to run away. Her plan was to stay with a girlfriend. Packing all her belongings into a shopping bag, Oprah headed for her girlfriend's home. To Oprah's surprise, no one was there. Oprah had forgotten to confirm the plan with her girlfriend. In too deep to turn back, Oprah aimlessly wandered the streets of Milwaukee, her shopping bag in hand.

Stopping to observe a limousine, she discovered singer Aretha Franklin stepping out of it. Suddenly hit with an inspired idea, a tearful Oprah quickly approached Aretha Franklin and hysterically announced that she had been abandoned and needed money to return home to Ohio. According to Oprah, Aretha was so convinced by her performance that she gave her one hundred dollars.

Oprah used the money to rent a room at a nearby hotel. With no one to keep her company, she had time to reflect on the situation she was in. As her money dwindled down to nothing, Oprah realized she had painted herself into a corner. She wanted to return home, but under the circumstances feared the wrath of her mother who, no doubt, had spent the week sick over her daughter's disappearance. With nowhere else to turn, Oprah sought the help of her minister.

The minister agreed to accompany Oprah home. Vernita Lee was livid—this time Oprah had gone too far. Deciding her eldest daughter needed to be taught a lesson, Vernita Lee took her down to juvenile hall. Fortunately for Oprah, there wasn't a spare bed available. Vernita Lee returned home with her daughter, but knew some major changes had to take place. Picking up the phone, she placed a call to Oprah's father.

3

Life with Father

"When my father took me, it changed the course of my life. H saved me. He simply knew what he wanted and expected. He would take nothing less."

"**G**rowing up, I acted differently when being raised by my mother than being raised with my father," Oprah has told her TV audience. "I would break curfew. I'd stay out. I'd run the streets. Because I knew I could get away with it. You know why? Because my mother would say, 'If you come in here late again, I'm gonna break your neck!' Well, I knew she wasn't gonna break my neck. So I would do whatever I could get away with. On the other hand, my father didn't even have to say it. You just knew that, if you did it, you'd be shot. You knew if you came in late you would die!" With that in mind, Oprah didn't even attempt to test her father's limits the way she did Vernita Lee's.

"I was a child who was always in need of discipline," Oprah confided to Joan Rivers. "I have a great father who used to tell me, 'Listen, girl, if I tell you a mosquito can pull a wagon, don't ask me no questions. Just hitch him up.' That's the kind of dad I had, who was a very, very stern disciplinarian. It's because of him, I believe, I am where I am today."

"She just wouldn't listen to her mother," Vernon told *People* magazine, as he explained why Vernita Lee turned a fourteen-year-old Oprah over to him and Zelma. "She needed some discipline to make sure she got a good start."

"I was badly in need of direction," admits Oprah.

Once Oprah arrived back in Nashville, Vernon expected immediate changes in her behavior, beginning with the bad habit she had picked up of calling him Pops. Vernon made it clear that he would continue to call her Oprah or Gail (her middle name), as he had when she lived with him, and she would continue to call him Daddy.

Oprah was also required to make adjustments in her appearance. Halter tops may have been acceptable for a well-developed teenage girl living in Milwaukee, but Vernon refused to have such a cheap, gaudy look cross his Nashville doorstep. Besides the halter tops, Oprah's short, tight skirts were packed away and replaced with more conservative clothing, such as blouses with buttons and longer, loose-fitting skirts. Like many young, inexperienced teenage girls, Oprah put on too much makeup. When Vernon caught her wearing it, he'd insist she wipe it off. He was determined to see his daughter return, not only in body, but also in spirit.

"When my father took me, it changed the course of my life," Oprah told *The Washington Post*. "He saved me. He simply knew what he wanted and expected. He would take nothing less."

Vernon and Zelma still live in the same house Oprah grew up in as a teenager. It's in a predominantly black, lower-middle-class neighborhood, where although not everyone necessarily knows one another on a first-name basis, there exists a real sense of community. Faith United, the church Vernon and Zelma belong to and where Vernon is a deacon, is not far from their home.

In 1964, Vernon opened his own business, a barbershop. He later expanded, opening a small grocery store adjacent to the barbershop. In 1975, he was elected to Nashville's Metro Council, representing the Fifth District, which has a population of fifteen thousand.

A small gas station is located near Vernon's barbershop. Down the road, on Interstate 65, is a string of inexpensive motels. The majority are open for legitimate travelers in search of shelter for the night; others operate under more dubious auspices, with prostitutes hustling nearby on the highway.

One of Vernon's first tasks upon Oprah's return was to teach her how to handle herself with boys. He explained frankly the various approaches boys would use to try and lure her into bed. He added that if she didn't hold herself up, the boys certainly weren't going to hold up for her.

When Vernita Lee sent Oprah to live with Vernon, her frustration in not being able to deal with her daughter may have stemmed from her fear that Oprah, because of her then-rebellious nature, was on her way to becoming an unwed teenage mother. Having been one herself, Vernita Lee was more than aware of the limitations such a position imposes on a teenage girl. Even Oprah has acknowledged that, while living in Milwaukee, chances were better than average that she could have ended up as another welfare statistic.

Not forgetting how close she came to realizing that possibility, Oprah has used her influence to try and lend guidance to a group of economically disadvantaged teenage girls who live in a Chicago housing project. Along with female members of her staff, as well as women who work at other Chicago TV stations, Oprah meets regularly with the girls. The possibility that any one of the teenagers could become pregnant is a major concern. Oprah related to Joan Barthel of Ms. magazine that she has told the girls, "Get pregnant and I'll break your face! Don't tell me you want to do great things in your life and still not be able to tell a boy no. You want something to love and to hug, tell me and I'll buy you a puppy!"

Vernon Winfrey was not studious as a young man, and in later life, realizing that a good education opens doors, he took it upon himself to set strict guidelines regarding Oprah's school performance. Above-average grades were expected from her. One of the first report cards Oprah brought home after returning to Nashville contained mostly C's. Vernon informed Oprah her report card was unacceptable. This confused Oprah: wasn't a C considered passing? Yes, agreed Vernon, and for an average student a C would be considered a tolerable grade. But, he added, Oprah possessed the ability to achieve higher grades and that's what he expected from her.

Vernon asked Oprah what kind of person she wanted to be in life. Before she answered, he explained that, as he saw it, there were three kinds of people in life. The first makes things happen, the second watches things happen, and the third, well, the third's not quite sure what's happening. Oprah decided immediately that she wanted nothing to do with the last two.

Zelma, meanwhile, resumed Oprah's ancillary home studies. Every two weeks they would visit the library and Oprah would select five books, which she not only had to read, but as before also write reports on. Oprah didn't mind the reading. It introduced her to such authors as Maya Angelou, who wrote what Oprah still cites as her favorite book, *I Know Why the Caged Bird Sings*, and Margaret Walker, who wrote *Jubilee*. What *did* pain Oprah was the limitations set on her TV viewing. Only one hour a day! Even worse, the hour was scheduled just before "Leave It to Beaver" came on!

Vernon never, as he put it, had to "whoop" Oprah. Instead, a stern look out of the corner of his eye, with his chin down on his chest, immediately made it clear to

Oprah what was expected of her and let her know it was time to straighten up. She said the discipline and guidance Vernon offered her "channeled my need for love and attention in a new direction."

Oprah attended Nashville's East High School. It no longer exists today; its doors closed forever in the mid-eighties. But in the late sixties, Oprah was one of the first blacks to help integrate East High's student body. What made this experience different for Oprah from her year at Nicolet in Milwaukee was that she was more in step economically with her fellow classmates.

As Oprah grew more comfortable and secure with the love offered by her father and stepmother, she became more confident at school, even becoming an active participant in its politics. She decided to run for student council president. Attending a recently integrated high school, Oprah realized her race could become an issue in the election and wisely sidestepped it. The platform she ran on touched the concerns of the entire student body. For starters she promised a more appetizing menu in the school cafeteria. She intended to improve school spirit. Finally, rather than have recorded music at the prom, Oprah promised a live band. When the votes were tabulated, she was announced the winner.

Oprah's natural gift as a communicator blossomed while at East High. She reveled in performing dramatic readings based on the lives of such historically famous black women as Sojourner Truth and Harriet Tubman. When Oprah was fifteen she visited California to speak to church groups. While in California, she had the opportunity to tour Hollywood for the first time. She ignored the seedy souvenir shops along Hollywood Boulevard and marveled at the names of all the famous actors she saw laid out before her on the sidewalks. Vernon told *The Nashville Banner* that when Oprah returned home from her Hollywood trip she told him, "Daddy, I got down on my knees there and ran my hand along all those stars on the street and I said to myself, 'One day, I'm going to put my own star among those stars.' "

"That was the foreshadowing I had that she would one day be famous," Vernon added.

For Oprah a glimpse into what her future held had come when she was twelve years old. While visiting Vernon in Nashville she was paid five hundred dollars to speak at a church. That night Oprah informed her father that what she wanted to do for a living was to be paid to talk. "I told my daddy then and there that I planned to be very famous."

Vernon modestly refuses to take credit for Oprah's success. "Oprah was born with a certain talent, a gift," he has said. "We just cultivated it as best we could."

When Oprah was seventeen she was invited by President Richard Nixon to attend the White House Conference on Youth in Estes Park, Colorado. Youths from all over the country, as well as five hundred business leaders, met to explore new approaches and develop recommendations on issues concerning the young. Oprah was also selected that year to represent East High as an Outstanding Teenager of America. She was chosen for her academic achievements and excellent community service. She won first place in the Tennessee District of the National Forensic League Tournament for her dramatic interpretation of Margaret Walker's *Jubilee*, and flew to Stanford University in Palo Alto, California, to compete with students from across the country.

While in high school Oprah, like most teenage girls, also discovered boys. When she was sixteen she had a passionate crush on a boy named Nathaniel. She wrote in her diary:

June 11, 1970
I blew it completely with Nathaniel. I was leaving for Kansas City for the speech tournament. He was going to give me his address so I could send him a

postcard. I was so thrilled that he called that I said,
"No, if you give it to me now you probably won't
call back." And he didn't.

July 9, 1970
I do wish Nathaniel would call. I'm still waiting.

July 10, 1970
Thoughts on Nathaniel. Knowing you will never
call does not stifle my desire for you. I shall always
remember you with a smile, Nathaniel, for you
taught me to be bold is to be lonely.

When Oprah was a senior in high school she started
dating Anthony Otey, voted most popular boy by his
class. It made sense that Oprah would date Anthony; she
had been voted most popular girl. Oprah and Anthony
shared other common interests. Whereas Oprah wanted
to grow up to become a famous actress, Anthony looked
forward to a life as a successful, acclaimed artist. His goal
was to "leave mankind an advancement in the field of
art." He was president of the Art Club and had also won
medals for his art work. Like Oprah, he was an honor
student who still found time for serious involvement in
student affairs. He and Oprah got their pictures in the
paper when they walked sixteen miles in a walkathon for
the March of Dimes. Their slogan was "Walk a mile for the
life of a child."

Anthony considered a note he received from Oprah,
written in multicolored Magic Marker and dated September 22, 1970, as the "start of the greatest thing that ever
happened to me." He had asked Oprah, whom, incidentally, he called Gail, if she would be interested in going
steady. In her letter, which was written while she sat in
Mr. Pate's government class, Oprah addressed Anthony's
request. But first she told him that she was feeling sick
inside because she had turned down a chance to partici-

pate in America's Junior Miss Pageant. In hindsight, she wrote, she wished she hadn't. She was also feeling miserable because a close friend, Norma Scruggs, wasn't speaking to her. Getting to the heart of the letter, Oprah informed Anthony that he would have to wait before receiving an answer to his offer about going steady. She didn't feel Mr. Pate's government class was the proper place to give such an important answer because the environment was just too "blah." She reasoned that she would probably remember their relationship, good or bad, for a long time and hated the thought that her memories of it might be clouded by the fact that she had said yes in East High's "blah" hallways. How undramatic can you get? she asked. In less than two years, Oprah had changed from a confused, rebellious teenager who stole money from her mother's purse into one who came close to resembling a real-life version of Gidget.

Anthony was a romantic, saving ticket stubs from movies and concerts they attended. Like other high-school couples in 1970, they cried through *Love Story*, cheered James Earl Jones on in *The Great White Hope*, and laughed hysterically at Redd Fox in *Cotton Comes to Harlem*. Shortly after Christmas they went to a local performance of *Hair*, then considered controversial because of its nudity, as well as its antiwar theme. Exactly one month before Oprah's seventeenth birthday they attended a Jackson Five concert at the Municipal Auditorium and were lucky enough to sit in the third row, close enough to actually see sweat pour off young Michael's brow. Years later, when the Jacksons would perform their Victory concert at Comiskey Park in Chicago, Oprah would be designated to introduce them before a crowd of fifty thousand cheering fans.

Expressions of the day for black students growing up in 1970 were "Right On!" "It's Your Thing!" "Sock It to Me!" "What It Mean?" "Say It Loud, I'm Black and I'm Proud!"

Hamburgers, a staple of the high-school student's diet, cost thirty-five cents. A Burger King Whopper went for sixty-five cents. Gasoline, which was vital to any student who had a car, cost twenty-seven cents a gallon. Popcorn at the movies cost fifty cents, including butter. Record albums cost a mere four dollars. Forty-fives, a necessary ingredient for any successful basement party, cost eighty-nine cents.

The civil rights movement, despite the violent assassination of Dr. King, was still going strong. Billboards in Nashville's black neighborhoods read, "It's time for black people, and all people of goodwill, to stamp out racism in Nashville. Help the Movement. Join the economic withdrawal."

Besides attending movies and concerts, Oprah and Anthony spent their dates hanging out at Pizza Hut or Burger King. Occasionally they would go bowling, or plan an afternoon of swimming at Old Hickory Lake. Sometimes they would take quiet walks, holding hands, through Shelby Park. When Anthony purchased his first car, a 1964 Comet, they would sometimes park at Shelby Park and discuss their futures, as well as engage in a little innocent necking.

At Christmas they exchanged gifts. Anthony surprised Oprah with a forty-inch-long orange St. Bernard stuffed animal—a dog of her own at last! She, in turn, presented Anthony with a SUPER BAD! knit shirt, which caused Anthony to proclaim, "She's the greatest!" A month later, Oprah celebrated her seventeenth birthday with a party held at East High's gym. The entire student body was invited. Oprah's early teenage years of feeling like an outsider were way behind her.

A year after Oprah's term as president of the student council ended, the editors of the East High newspaper blasted their fellow students for their apathy in regard to school spirit. They wrote, "The environment of East has become like a river in the past two years. At first it was a river of friendship. But it has gradually acquired a rough surface, which none of us has been able to overcome. It is not completely the fault of the students. But we have contributed to the achievement of this environment."

Oprah, however, was far from becoming labeled an apathetic student at East High. She was elected to the prom decorating committee. Anthony served as its president. The school newspaper described the theme of their prom as an "Evening above the clouds." It explained that the theme would be carried out by decorating and enclosing the gym on all sides with backdrops of cityscapes and clouds. Clouds were going to be attached around tables in the gym. Two large white columns were to be placed at the bottom of the gym's stairs, which, incidentally, would be decorated to resemble a stairway ascending into the clouds. Blue, silver, and white paper with suspended stars would cover the gym's lower ceiling. It was exactly the kind of prom you could easily imagine Archie Andrews and his pals, Betty and Veronica, enthusiastically planning at the fictional Riverdale High.

The prom announcement read:

The Senior Class
of
East Nashville Senior High School
Presents
"An Evening Above the Clouds"
High School Gymnasium
Friday Evening
May Seventh
Nineteen Hundred Seventy-one
Senior Class Motto:
"We've Only Just Begun"
Music Provided by:
Don Q. Pullen & Band

51

Before heading for their prom, Oprah and Anthony stopped at a restaurant called Mario's for dinner. Since this was the most special night of their high-school years, they decided to go all out in ordering their meal. For appetizers they had cheese, olives, and celery. The main course was scampi, with French bread and Italian spaghetti. The beverage was iced tea.

Later, on their way to East High's gym, they experienced car trouble. Fortunately, Anthony managed to clear up the problem and they arrived at their prom fashionably late. Since it was a special night, Vernon temporarily rescinded Oprah's usual midnight curfew. Anthony brought her home at 3:15 A.M. Anthony later recalled, "It was truly an evening above the clouds . . . I'm still afloat with memories of it."

Like most high-school romances, Oprah's and Anthony's was a fleeting one. Separate interests were responsible for their drifting apart shortly after graduation. Oprah, in the spring of her senior year, had embarked on a new and exciting career that would take up most of her free time.

4

First Radio Job

"I said I wanted to be a journalist because I was interested in having people understand the truth, so they could better understand themselves. And the judges asked, 'Well, what kind of journalist?' and I answered, 'Barbara Walters.' "

While looking for people to sponsor her in the March of Dimes walkathon, Oprah wandered into the studios of Nashville radio station WVOL, which were near her home. Since it was early afternoon and most of the station's employees were out to lunch, Oprah had difficulty finding someone at the station willing to put up money for her walk. Just as Oprah was about to leave the station, John Heidelberg, WVOL's affable and friendly disk jockey, was returning from lunch. A station employee quickly asked Oprah to wait a minute. Introducing John to Oprah, she said, "Maybe he can help you."

With a winning smile and a confident manner, Oprah

explained to John why she was at the station. "I asked her what the walkathon was all about," John recalls. "She explained that she walked so many miles and I would have to pay for the number of miles she walked. That was pretty much all there was to it. I told her, 'Sure, I'll do it.'" Successful at finding another sponsor, Oprah left the station beaming. Meanwhile, John went on the air and immediately put the incident out of his head.

A few weeks later Oprah returned to WVOL and told John, "Well, I'm here to collect the money." Suddenly remembering that he had, in fact, pledged to support her walk, John willingly paid her. Oprah's second encounter with John left an impression.

"I admired her voice," he says. "She was very articulate. Her grammar was very good." This struck a chord with John, who prided himself on being articulate and using good grammar whenever possible. "I'm from outside the boondocks of Mississippi," he continues. "The concept and image that people get of blacks living in the South can sometimes be very negative. I watched an old Western when I was a young man and was very impressed by a gentleman in it who could speak very well. I said, 'Someday I'll do that.' I just liked hearing that in people. And Oprah had it. I thought, 'Hey, here's a young lady who can go places.'"

John asked Oprah if she had ever considered a career in broadcasting. "She hadn't given it any thought at all. But the voice was there."

John told Oprah about the qualities he felt she possessed and asked if she would be interested in possibly working in radio. He then asked Oprah if she would be willing to make a tape for him. Oprah responded, "Sure."

"I took her into the newsroom. I ripped some copy off the news wire and asked her to read it. I told her that way I'd have something to show the station manager so he could hear what she sounded like."

Stepping up to a mike, Oprah read the copy. Listening to her, John observed that, besides having a rich, deep, clear voice, Oprah had another quality that was vital for anyone who wanted to succeed in radio. "Radio's a companion," he explains. "People out there listening want that person on the radio to be warm, affectionate. They want that person to talk to them, not at them. The listener wants to relate. He wants to be able to say, 'Hey, that's my friend. I know him.' He can call him up and say, 'Hey, Buddy, this is so and so.' The guy knows Buddy. He may not have seen him, but he knows him like he's his friend." John saw in Oprah her potential for being the listener's friend. "She had a very warm personality." Taking Oprah's tape, John promised to let WVOL's station manager, Noble Blackwell, listen to it and said he would get back to her. John envisioned Oprah doing newscasts.

At that time, however, during the early seventies, women, for the most part, were still relegated to offering female listeners recipes and household hints. "It was hard for women to get into radio," John recalls. When the FCC required radio stations to begin affirmative action programs, things began to change. "Station managers hired them because they needed a minority. They felt like, 'Well, we've gotta protect our license, so we'll hire some females.'"

"At that time, WVOL was a training ground," recalls Dana Davidson, who, like Oprah, got her start at WVOL. She has been with the station since the late sixties.

"We had a lot of females who came through," adds John. WVOL, which appealed mainly to black listeners, was, in the early seventies, a black-operated but white-owned station. "We were a training ground for a lot of young blacks who otherwise wouldn't have had a chance to make it in radio."

"Back in those days," says Dana, "on-the-air training was not a rare thing to happen in radio. Now, most of our announcers come in from broadcasting schools."

John played Oprah's demo tape for Noble Blackwell and he said, "That does sound pretty good." When he played the demo for other people in management at WVOL, however, they were less optimistic about Oprah's potential. After all, they reasoned, she's only a seventeen-year-old kid. "But I convinced them that here was a young lady who had a lot of the things we were looking for and to give her a break," says John. "Eventually, we did give her a break."

Oprah was hired to work part-time on the weekends doing news. But it took some convincing to persuade Vernon to let his daughter work at WVOL. "He was skeptical about a lot of things," says John. "And I could understand why. You have a daughter, you want to protect her. Was she going to be out there all by herself?" Not to mention the reputation disk jockeys had for being womanizers. What kind of environment was a radio station for a decent young girl? asked Vernon. "We deejays at radio stations do have some bad reputations," admits John. "We're all accused of womanizing. But Mr. Winfrey knew I was married at the time. The people at WVOL convinced him that I was a pretty decent guy. Once we assured him that she would be in good hands, that nobody was going to abuse her, or mistreat her in any way, he came around."

"Vernon Winfrey did a great job raising her," notes John. "What she is today is a testament to him. Of course, back then, she thought he was a little too strict on her at times. He didn't want her involved in the wrong crowd. He didn't want her hanging around a whole lot of guys, or a whole lot of guys hanging around her. He looked at his daughter and he wanted her to achieve something in life." Though Vernon wanted to protect her from what he thought was a dangerously promiscuous atmosphere, WVOL was actually the best place for Oprah to be to start making her career achievements.

"John really did discover Oprah," says Dana.

"I feel like I was a catalyst. I'm sure she would've made it at one point or another. You just don't hold that kind of talent back," acknowledges John. "I feel good knowing I had a hand in shaping some things."

"You don't just go into radio and start performing. You go through a training period," explains Dana, discussing WVOL's policy for hiring undeveloped talent. For the first few weekends Oprah worked at WVOL she didn't receive a salary. John kept her busy teaching her the basics. "At that time there was nothing outstanding that would make you think there was anything out of the ordinary. She was an average employee."

"Ope knew that she had something on the ball," says John. "She didn't feel intimidated or threatened by anything. That was one of the things that caught my eye. It was like she wasn't worried about anything. Nothing bothered her."

"She was aggressive," adds Dana. "Not at all shy. She knew where she was going."

After a few short weeks at WVOL, Oprah was receiving a weekly salary of a hundred dollars. In addition to performing newscasts at the station on the weekends, Oprah started coming in for a few hours weekdays after school. She joked to a reporter that one of the reasons she accepted the job at WVOL was because, without "Leave It to Beaver" to watch in the afternoon, it gave her something to do.

Being new in radio and still a high-school student, Oprah occasionally felt insecure about her ability to perform well. "There were times when she was a little despondent," acknowledges John. "I remember once I had to sit and talk with her because she was almost on the verge of tears. There were one or two people within the station that felt she didn't sound good. She took it personally.

"I'd tell her, 'Don't let those people get you down. You've got what it takes. This is just a learning process. If anyone says anything it's because they're jealous.' I'd give her pep talks. I'd tell her how great she sounded. And she did.

Eventually, she got to the point where she started believing it, and realized that these people weren't trying to do anything but pull her down."

"Oprah was one who wanted to excel and take advantage of the opportunities that were given her," recalls Dana. "And I think she made some up on her own. It wasn't always easy for her."

Dana also says that Oprah was more than willing to offer her time to good causes. "We had a local organization we called Project: HELP. We had several people in the community who were on kidney machines and needed money to help defray their costs. Oprah worked very closely with us on that. She was eager to participate."

At a church gospel program, Oprah offered to perform a dramatic reading of a piece written by a black poet. Watching Oprah perform, Dana says, "was so very breathtaking. She portrayed the part so vividly."

One of Oprah's major goofs while working at WVOL happened when she accidentally left her mike on while talking to her boyfriend. At the time she was dating a young man named William Taylor. John remembers that "Taylor had a pretty good image." Even Vernon approved of him.

When John was promoted to program director at WVOL, Oprah convinced him to give William a chance at the station. "She cared about him a great deal," recalls John. Willing to give anyone interested a chance, John hired William to work part-time at the station. But William didn't possess the same potential Oprah demonstrated and didn't stay with the station very long. "He wasn't an Oprah," says John.

"60 Minutes" later filmed Oprah talking to an audience of teenage girls about William. She told them, "I have been in the backseat with some Negro with his hand on my breast talking about, 'Baby, you don't have to' in one breath and the next minute saying, 'If you love me you would.' But had I not said no I could be in a position that never would have allowed me to be able to do the things, be all that I can be, like right now, because when I was seventeen, Lord, if William Taylor had've married me, I'd have been married. To a mortician, because that's what he is.

"I'd be married to a mortician and probably teaching Sunday school in Nashville someplace because I wanted him. Lord, I wanted him. Threw his keys down the toilet. I wanted him. Stood in front of the door and threatened to jump off the balcony if he didn't stay. I wanted him. I was on my knees begging him, 'Please don't go, please don't go!' To this day I thank God he left."

A week after the "60 Minutes" segment on Oprah aired, a letter was read from William Taylor saying he didn't realize Oprah felt so strongly for him.

Oprah told Lyn Tornabene of *Woman's Day*, "My father always said, 'When you fall, you fall so hard.' And it seemed to be true. I'd fall for some guy and it would be life or death."

Shortly after Oprah started working at WVOL, the station manager's house burned down. Impressed by the fire department's swiftness in trying to douse the blaze, Blackwell decided to have WVOL participate in the upcoming Miss Fire Prevention contest. Several Nashville radio stations selected a candidate, usually a red-haired teenage girl, to represent them in the contest. The winner would speak at schools and to various civic organizations, giving tips on how to prevent fires. The program was sponsored by the Nashville Fire Department.

Blackwell's secretary suggested that Oprah represent WVOL in the contest. Blackwell agreed and his secretary told John, "You've gotten Oprah a job in radio, why don't you sponsor her in the Miss Fire Prevention contest?"

John said, "Well, sure, I'll do that." He recalls that they had a hard time convincing Vernon to let Oprah participate in the contest. Finally, her father agreed, but he specifically asked that John escort her to the contest, which was held at the Holiday Inn.

"Lo and behold," says John, "she won the darned thing."

Oprah told Audrey Edwards of *Essence* magazine, "I know it's not a biggie, but I was the only black—the first black—to win."

"The crowd was just overwhelmed with her," recalls John. "And you could see that she was just loving every minute of it."

Oprah later told Barbara Walters that the reason she won the contest was because she told them she wanted to grow up to be Barbara Walters. Originally, she was going to answer that she wanted to become a fourth-grade schoolteacher, but having seen Barbara Walters on television that morning, she suddenly changed her mind. She said, "I said I wanted to be a journalist because I was interested in having people understand the truth, so they could better understand themselves. And the judges asked, 'Well, what kind of journalist?' and I answered, 'Barbara Walters.'"

John remembers that Oprah was especially surprised to have newspaper cameramen rushing to take her picture. He felt her attitude was, "Hey, I love this! This is great! This is going places!"

"Being black, and being brought up in the South, that's sometimes considered a handicap," says Dana. "But sometimes it also serves as a purpose for you to make a better life for yourself. We haven't always had it easy, but there's always that feeling in the back of your mind that you can do it if you want to."

For Oprah, landing a job at WVOL and winning the Miss Fire Prevention contest was only a small glimpse of what was to come.

5

College Days and Beauty Pageants

"People see me and they see that I am black. That's something I celebrate. But I don't feel it's something I need to wave a banner about, which used to cause me all kinds of problems in college. I was not a dashiki-wearing kind of woman."

After graduating from East High School, Oprah spent the summer working part-time at WVOL. When fall arrived she decided to continue working part-time at the radio station, while registering full-time as a student at Tennessee State University, located less than seven miles from her father's home. Oprah had considered attending an out-of-state college, to experience a new lifestyle, but Vernon was dead set against it. He convinced Oprah to enroll at TSU because he thought she could receive just as good an education there as anyplace else.

The late Dr. Thomas E. Poag, founder of TSU's speech-theater department, was familiar with Oprah's dramatic talents and was anxious to have her as a student at TSU. Dr. Poag was famous for being the first black to receive a master's and Ph.D. in theater arts in the United States. "He was very much in love with Oprah's performances," recalls Dr. William Cox, who taught at TSU for over thirty-six years.

With Dr. Poag's influence, Oprah decided to major in speech and drama at TSU. "I was a frustrated actress," she says. "I majored in speech and drama with the hopes of becoming an actress." Vernon wasn't entirely pleased with Oprah's choice of major, but figured since she was willing to compromise and attend TSU, he could learn to live with her decision.

Dr. Cox first met Oprah during freshman week. He got to know her better when she enrolled in a class he taught called Theater Practice. "When she came here she was very much matured," says Dr. Cox. "She knew what she wanted and where she was going. I guess that's one of the reasons we got along so well."

Dr. Cox recalls that Oprah would attend classes during the early part of the day, then head for her part-time job at WVOL in the afternoon. "As a matter of fact, the station was located between the school and her home. We used to tease Oprah because she was on only during the day." Vernon's reputation as a strict father was well-known among the staff at TSU. When Oprah started having problems with her car lights and was unable to drive at night, the faculty jokingly speculated that Vernon had taken the fuses out of Oprah's car so that she would have to be home before dark. "Supposedly, he was gonna fix them," says Dr. Cox, laughing.

Dr. Jamie Williams, who taught oral interpretation at TSU for more than thirty years, immediately recognized that Oprah possessed qualities necessary for succeeding in the performing arts. "She was a very outgoing, enthusiastic young lady. I emphasize every day in my speech class that one of the important ingredients in communication is enthusiasm. I tell them that is not only true in speaking, that's true for success in life. Oprah had that kind of enthusiasm. She also always had a kind of intellectual curiosity about things."

Oprah has said her years at TSU weren't happy ones. It was the early seventies and a large number of black students behaved militantly, sporting large afros as a symbol of black pride and organizing boycotts on campus against race discrimination. "It was a pretty big movement here at that time," says Dr. Cox. "Like all the other campuses."

Because Oprah didn't openly participate in protests, she was criticized by some students, who believed she should have been more actively involved. Oprah told *People* magazine, "I refused to conform to the militant thinking of the time. I hated, hated, hated college. Now I bristle when somebody comes up and says they went to Tennessee State with me. Everybody was angry for four years. It was an all-black college, and it was very *in* to be angry. Whenever there was any conversation on race, I was on the other side, maybe because I never felt the kind of repression other black people are exposed to. I think I was called 'nigger' once, when I was in fifth grade."

"She was criticized and pretty much condemned on campus," acknowledges Dr. Cox. "Many of us were aware of what the male black leaders were doing. They were leading these kids here and there and then, of course, dating white girls at night. We were very much aware of it, especially the black women."

Dr. Cox, however, adds that *People*'s coverage of Oprah's college years was sensationalized. "Negative journalism is what I think it is." Referring to the quotes attributed to Oprah about her years as a student at TSU in *People*, he says, "I'm very disappointed in Oprah making that statement, if, indeed, she did make it that blunt. I think she could have been more diplomatic."

Oprah told Mike Wallace on "60 Minutes," "People see me

and they see that I am black, that's something that I celebrate. But I don't feel that it's something that I need to wave a banner about, which used to cause me all kinds of problems in college. I was not a dashiki-wearing kind of woman."

"Oprah's a very honest and open woman," says Dr. Williams. "If she says she was not angry during that period she was at TSU, she's just telling it like it is. There are always gonna be a bunch of people who try to set limitations on how we view ourselves and how we perceive problems. To expect everybody who is black to be a civil rights activist, that's not the way human beings are. When we jump on our own people because they do not conform to our image of what they ought to be, or how we ought to perform, we do people a disservice."

What troubled Dr. Cox about the *People* article was that a reporter from the magazine had interviewed him. "Nothing I said came out in it." Dr. Cox decided it was because "I only had positive material to share about Oprah."

"In fact," he continues, "I get concerned that no one knows about her experience at TSU in theater. I think most people get the idea that her first major acting move was in *The Color Purple*. But Oprah did a great deal of theater within our department. Even with the church she belonged to here. She was a wonderful church worker. She had a young group that called themselves Sweet Honey in the Rock. I think every Sunday they were booked in a church with their program, with dramatic readings from *God's Trombones* by James Johnson. It was a one-woman drama with a group of religious singers backing her up. I think she knew every bit of poetry in *God's Trombones*. I never see anything like this in print. It bothers me."

One of Dr. Williams's most vivid memories of Oprah's talent as an actress is when Oprah performed a monologue from *Jubilee*. "Whenever I hear Oprah," she says now, "I hear her doing that piece from *Jubilee*. It was a speech that says you've really got to be a loving and caring human being. You've gotta be capable of forgiving people, no matter what they do to you. It's a kind of notion that isn't very popular today. It's probably what Oprah believes." Dr. Williams laughs fondly. "She was a joy. Students thoroughly enjoyed coming to class and listening to her."

Dr. Williams points out that someone once said to her that she must be very proud of what she had done with Oprah. "I said I didn't have anything to do with Oprah's success. I'm not taking any credit for her ability in oral interpretation. She has a natural talent. Obviously, for her to interpret pieces she has to work on them. But *she* has to work on them. A teacher can stand back and say, 'I think you ought to try this,' or 'Have you thought about doing that?' But, basically, a person such as Oprah has the natural talent and probably would have been just as good in oral interpretation without ever having had to take a course in it. As her teacher I do not intend to try and grab any credit for what she has become, except to say that I am delighted."

"Somebody tried to lay it on me that she has that heavy voice," says Dr. Cox, referring to Oprah's rich, deep voice. "But I said when I met Oprah she was talking baritone. She's had that voice ever since I've known her."

Dr. Cox recalls the only full-length play in which Oprah performed at TSU. "She played Coretta King in a play that was in competition nationally." It was an original play, written by a TSU student and based on the life of Dr. Martin Luther King, Jr. "To show you how strict her father was, when we were doing *The Martin Luther King Story*, Dr. Poag had to all but beg her father to allow her to perform in it because we rehearsed from seven to nine o'clock at night. Dr. Poag even offered to carry her home after rehearsals. I know that would've been a sacrifice for my friend Dr. Poag. But her father gave his consent.

"She had an enjoyable time, I'm sure, with our group. We spent a month on the production and had no problems. She

65

was always on time, always knew her lines. She never said a word while we were painting or nailing the sets when she was trying to do her lines."

Dr. Cox recalls that Oprah was close friends with her costar in the production, Alonzo Ward, who played Dr. King. "He wasn't her boyfriend," he points out. "He was a companion. Both of them had shaky beginnings, but both found their way. He was shyer than Oprah." Dr. Cox laughs when he recalls a minor dispute Oprah and Alonzo had over Oprah's choice of accessories for her part as Coretta King. "One night she came in wearing high-heel shoes. Alonzo wasn't as tall as Oprah and was very much alarmed about the situation. He felt Coretta King shouldn't overshadow her husband by being taller than he was. Eventually, they worked it out."

Oprah also participated in a drama conference sponsored by the National Association of Speech and Arts, representing TSU, which brought her to Chicago. The drama department succeeded in receiving Vernon's consent to let Oprah go by assuring him that responsible adults, such as Dr. Cox, would be chaperoning the students during their stay in Chicago.

The conference was held at Kennedy-King College, an all-black city college on Chicago's South Side, a high-crime area. A number of the buildings in the neighborhood were boarded up, abandoned by their owners. What troubled the students, particularly Oprah, was that the motel where they stayed during their visit was within walking distance of the college. With the exception of the street signs to indicate they were in Chicago, Oprah could just as easily have been back in the Milwaukee neighborhood where she had spent the early part of her adolescence. At night the students were kept awake by trains passing through the area. Loud, boisterous, inebriated patrons of the several bars surrounding the motel, many of which stayed open until 4 A.M., also interrupted their sleep.

Awakening in the early morning to shower and prepare for the drama conference, the students unhappily discovered that the motel also had serious plumbing problems. "There was no hot water after seven o'clock in the morning to take baths," Dr. Cox recalls. Despite the challenging conditions the students confronted during their brief stay in Chicago, Oprah successfully managed to come in second at the conference with a dramatic reading from Ntozake Shange's *For Colored Girls Who Have Considered Suicide When the Rainbow Is Enuf.*

In addition to working part-time at WVOL her first three years at TSU, Oprah discovered another way to finance her college education. She entered, and won, beauty pageants. At the time, Oprah wasn't overweight but had to struggle to maintain her figure. Her participation in the pageants was partly influenced by the success and acclaim she encountered winning the Miss Fire Prevention title.

In March 1972, Oprah was crowned winner of the first Miss Black Nashville pageant, which was held at the Negro Elks Club. Winning the title meant Oprah would represent Nashville in the first Miss Black Tennessee pageant, scheduled in June.

The Miss Black Tennessee pageant was held at the National Guard Armory, where Oprah competed against six other contestants. When Oprah was announced the winner, it apparently came as quite a surprise to everyone. "I didn't expect to win, nor did anybody else expect me to," Oprah told Audrey Edwards of *Essence* magazine, "because there were all these vanillas [light-skinned girls] and here I was a fudge child. And Lord, were they upset, and I was upset for them, really I was. I said, 'Beats me, girls, I'm as shocked as you are. I don't know how I won, either.' "

Oprah's surprise at winning was a carryover from the conditioning she received as a child growing up in Milwaukee. Despite the fact that people did, in fact, find Oprah attractive, she couldn't believe it herself. Even today, if someone compliments Oprah on her attractiveness, she has a hard time accepting it. Regarding her winning the Miss Black Tennessee title, Oprah told Joan Barthel of *Ms.* magazine, "I won on poise and talent. I was raised to believe that the lighter your skin, the better you were. I wasn't light-skinned, so I decided to be the best and the smartest."

As the winner of the first Miss Black Tennessee pageant, Oprah was awarded a scholarship and an all-expense-paid trip to Hollywood, where the pageant would be held in August. Oprah's second trip to Hollywood would be considerably different from the first one she made. This time she wouldn't be rubbing her hand along the stars on Hollywood Boulevard's sidewalks as she considered the possibility of becoming famous one day. Instead, as a contestant in the Miss Black America pageant, Oprah would actually be meeting stars.

Entering the Miss Black America pageant, however, took on new ramifications for Oprah. Running on poise and talent in a local pageant is well and fine, but in a national competition, where she would be competing against contestants who grew up on the East and West Coasts, the stakes changed considerably. These were contestants who realized poise and talent had a place in the competition, but they also understood the importance of highlighting their own natural beauty. For Oprah, this created conflicts. "I think Oprah was not looking at that pageant as being a beauty pageant," says Dr. Janet Burch, a Nashville psychologist who was appointed to chaperon Oprah at the Miss Black America pageant.

"I didn't see Oprah as a person who was a typical beauty contestant," says Dr. Burch. "Most of the time, beauty contestants want to show off their physical attributes. You know, their looks, their body. Oprah wanted to maximize talent, her stability, her composure, her ability to answer questions. She completely minimized her physical attraction. That's just very unusual for a person who enters a beauty pageant."

Speaking of her participation in the pageant, Oprah told Sugar Rautbord of *Interview* magazine, "All of that was preparation for being where I am now. Being able to lose your sense of inhibition in front of crowds, and being able to talk to people about anything, and feeling very comfortable with yourself. All of those things helped me to be more comfortable with Oprah now, and this is what I'm selling."

Since this was the early seventies, blacks were redefining how they viewed themselves. The Miss America pageant, which still clung to dated values and conceptions of the ideal woman, didn't interest young black women. "There was a thrust among black Americans for a new image of beauty queens," says Dr. Burch. "It wasn't the fair hair, or the fine features, that served as a suggestion of beauty for blacks."

Dr. Burch recalls shopping with Oprah. "I guess we went out four or five times to get her wardrobe together to go to the Miss Black America pageant." She says that Oprah shied away from items that were colorful and striking. "She was far more interested in purchasing things that were plain, that really did not draw attention to her physical appearance. I know that she had a very nice figure and she was very attractive, smooth-complex-ioned, long hair, and considerably fewer pounds than she has now. The things that she chose were things that specifically made her look older, more sedate, more ca-reer-girlish looking." After a lot of encouragement, Oprah reluctantly agreed, up to a point, to compromise and go along with some of the suggestions Dr. Burch and the salesclerks made.

Although Oprah weighed less than she does today, even at the time of the pageant she wrestled with her weight. "It was something she constantly was watching," says Dr. Burch. "She had indicated that she knew she had to drop some weight before she went to California. She worked very hard on that. And she did look very nice."

In fact, of the contestants entered in the pageant, Oprah

was considered to have the nicest figure. This made her choice of bathing suit for the swimsuit competition all the more frustrating for her sponsors. The garment Oprah selected could just as easily have been a uniform for a girls' high-school swimming team. Dr. Burch describes it as "very, very plain."

Work kept Dr. Burch from arriving in Hollywood until two days after Oprah. Gordon Brown, director of the Miss Black Tennessee pageant, excitedly informed Dr. Burch that Oprah was the talk of the pageant. "They were saying that she was really so composed, that she would be a shoo-in," says Dr. Burch. "It had to do with her voice and her manner, and the fact that, probably, the other girls were trying too hard. They probably were trying to get attention or trying to be flashy." Armed with Gordon Brown's news, Dr. Burch was convinced "that this thing was in the bag!"

As chaperon, Dr. Burch's role was to help Oprah with the pageant itinerary, to see what was scheduled for her, where she had to be. Dr. Burch says she had very little to do with assisting Oprah on how to conduct herself at the pageant. "By the time you get to be something like Miss Black Tennessee, you already have quite a bit of instruction on how to carry yourself. It's more how to handle stress, how to keep your composure, how to get people to see you in the way you want to be seen. At that level the girls can be so stressful. At the local pageant, most of the girls know one another. Even at the state level you may know two or three other girls. On the national level, the chances are you're not going to know anybody there, and nobody there is going to know you."

Much of Oprah's week in Hollywood was spent rehearsing for the pageant, things such as the program's prologue and epilogue. Evenings were spent dining at a different, plush restaurant each night. There were also parties, where celebrities such as singer Bill Withers and

70

Denise Nicholson, a regular who appeared on ABC's "Room 222," mingled with the contestants. Dr. Burch recalls that Oprah's attitude toward meeting the celebrities was "Good to meet you, and I'm gonna be there with you one day!"

Since there was such a compression of time, it was important that the contestants present themselves in the best possible light at every opportunity. "The first impression tends to be the lasting impression," says Dr. Burch. "Oprah made good impressions because of the way she was able to conduct and handle herself. She did not go off on tangents. She was very goal-oriented. She set goal objectives for herself."

Like most people who knew Oprah at early stages of her growth, Dr. Burch immediately recognized her potential to succeed in life. "I never questioned for one minute that she would do well. I have never seen anybody who wanted to do well as much as Oprah did. She used to talk about things, like how one day she was going to be very, very, very wealthy. The thought always precedes the happening. If you really think you're going to be very wealthy, and very popular, and prominent, and you sincerely believe it, it's going to happen. You see, some people say it, but they don't really believe it. She believed it. People say, 'I'd like to be wealthy.' Oprah said, 'I'm going to be wealthy.' "

Dr. Burch says that Oprah also told her that she was going to be a big TV personality. "She didn't say 'I want to be,' or 'I would like to be,' she said, 'I'm going to be.' "

"Oprah had a knack," she continues. "She was bold enough to seek the information she wanted to know. I think a lot of times people are afraid to seek all the information they need in order to move ahead, make a decision, or whatever. Oprah had no qualms about asking anybody for anything."

For the talent competition Oprah had arranged a routine that would display her dramatic ability, as well as show off her singing voice. "She had a very beautiful voice," says Dr. Burch. "She sounded like Marian Anderson." For the routine, Oprah planned to enter dressed like an old, poor woman, wearing a bandanna wrapped around her head. After performing her monologue she intended to segue to a song, "Sometimes I Feel Like a Motherless Child." "We had suggested that she shed the old clothing," says Dr. Burch, "that she have on a solid, black, long-sleeved, long-legged leotard underneath. We figured maybe she could make the old-folks clothes kind of loose, that she could pull some strings to shed them, with this black leotard, so that she would just be a silhouette, and sing the song. It would be a drastic contrast." After a lot of prompting, Oprah agreed to the idea.

The night of the pageant, Dr. Burch also persuaded Oprah, after much difficulty, to try wearing her hair on top of her head. Dr. Burch felt this would lend height to Oprah and make her look very sophisticated. The sponsors also suggested Oprah have her face made up. Oprah had also brought with her an attractive and colorful gown that would show off the great figure revealed by the loss of the pounds she had worked so hard to shed. Everything was going like clockwork, until the pageant began.

The contestants came out wearing their gowns and, lo and behold, Oprah wasn't wearing the one Dr. Burch and the Miss Black Tennessee sponsors had expected. Nor was her hair piled high on her head. "Her hair was down and she had a limited amount of makeup," recalls Dr. Burch.

The gown Oprah wore? "I think it was the gown she wore at her high-school prom. It had a lot of ruffles." Dr. Burch says it made Oprah look like a sixteen-year-old high-school girl. "For the Nashville scene, that kind of dress may be all right," explains Dr. Burch. "But when you are entering a national competition, with people from the East Coast and West Coast, they typically tend to be more sophisticated in their choice of clothes."

But Oprah wasn't finished with her surprises. When the talent competition rolled around, Oprah entered, as previously arranged, wearing the old-woman clothing, and with the bandanna wrapped around her head. She performed her monologue to a hushed, enraptured audience. The piano began playing the first few chords of "Sometimes I Feel Like a Motherless Child" and Oprah began singing, without shedding her costume! "I don't think Oprah had ever really intended to," says Dr. Burch. "We were very surprised because we felt she really was going to do these things. I was astonished."

The finalists were announced and Oprah wasn't even in the running. Discussing the Miss Black America pageant with Luther Young of *The Baltimore Sun*, Oprah said she didn't do well at all and then added, "The girl from California who stripped won."

"I saw Oprah in a situation where she had some real ambivalence," says Dr. Burch. "On the one hand, she really wanted to be Miss Black America. But, on the other hand, she only wanted to be it if she could be it based on her calm and composure and the ability to answer questions. Oprah did not have the image of herself that she was glamorous. Her talent certainly showed off her best attributes."

"I would always win on the talent part," Oprah told *Essence*, "which was usually a dramatic reading. I could—I still can—hold my own easily."

"Her talent was good," acknowledges Dr. Burch. "But I think, in my opinion, that she never came across on stage as glamorous. If she had come across as glamorous she would've won."

Anyone who has ever had experience with beauty pageants will tell you that the contestants possess two personalities. There's what's known as the "front stage" personality, which the public witnesses as the contestants proudly show themselves off, shoulders back, heads held high, and all smiles. Then there's what's known as the "backstage" personality. This is where, once the pageant's over, the losing contestants let it all hang out; their insecurities, after a week of repression, become unmasked. Dr. Burch recalls that when she and the Miss Black Tennessee sponsors traveled backstage to congratulate Oprah on her performance they were surrounded by some very upset, tearful contestants. Minutes earlier the public had seen these very same young women rushing to hug Miss Black California and, through smiles, tearfully wishing her hearty congratulations on her victory.

Oprah emerged from the crowd of contestants perfectly composed. To the surprise of Dr. Burch and the sponsors, she was wearing, of all things, the colorful and striking gown she had carried with her to Hollywood. "She looked just simply smashing in it," notes Dr. Burch. Oprah gracefully accepted their compliments, but made no reference to the switch she had made in gowns. Nor did she mention her loss. Her attitude was, "Hey, we've got a party to go to!"

"I was sort of dumbfounded by it all," says Dr. Burch. "I had a sense it was almost relief. It was almost like she was glad she was in it, liked being in a position where she may win." Speaking of Oprah's loss, she adds, "She didn't really register it was real disappointment. I think to have won probably would have put her in more uncomfortable situations because she would probably have had to be flashier. Winning that pageant's like a hot potato. It was something she wanted, because it might help her career, but not wanted because she probably didn't want to play that role."

Later, Dr. Burch asked Oprah why she had changed her mind and not carried through on the plans they had arranged. "I remember her saying to me, 'I don't really see myself that way.' Then I remember her saying something to the effect that it might have given some displeasure to her father, that portraying that kind of image may not have been very pleasing to him."

Returning to Nashville, Dr. Burch had an opportunity to meet with Vernon. He thanked her for looking out for Oprah while she was in Hollywood and Dr. Burch mentioned what had happened. "I told him I really thought she could've won it hands down. He laughed and said, 'That has nothing to do with me. That's Oprah. That's just the way she is. Oprah makes her own decisions.' That's my point when I say she was very much her own person."

The following September Oprah resumed her studies at TSU. A year later she received a job offer she wasn't quite sure she was ready to accept.

6

First TV Job

"I was a token, but I was a happy, paid token."

In the fall of 1973, Oprah was asked to audition for a position at WTV-TV. "We were looking for an anchorperson at the time," says Chris Clark, news director and anchorperson at WTV. Chris was familiar with Oprah's work at WVOL, and he asked her if she'd be interested in auditioning for the station.

Before scheduling an appointment for an audition, Oprah went to John Heidelberg at WVOL. "She told me that Chris Clark had asked if she would mind coming over and trying out for a position at Channel 5. She asked me what I thought. She felt she'd be letting us down if she went for it. I told her, 'No, you go as far as your talent will take you. You have what it takes and don't look back.' "

Oprah later told her TV audience, "When I did my first audition for my first television job, I was such a nervous wreck, I had no idea what to do or say. And I thought in my head that maybe I'll just pretend I'm Barbara Walters. I will sit like Barbara, I will hold my head like Barbara. So I crossed my legs at the ankles, and I put my little finger under my chin, and I leaned across the desk, and I pretended to be Barbara Walters."

Hearing Oprah's story, Barbara Walters told her, "Thank goodness you got the job!"

Chris Clark says that when he saw Oprah's audition tape, "It didn't dawn on me she was imitating Barbara Walters. I don't think it came across that way. She may have used that to psych herself up for it. But she came across as Oprah Winfrey." Laughing, Chris adds, "That was the charm of it. She came across as herself.

"If you have seen as many audition tapes as I have, I've seen people do their David Brinkleys, I've seen them do their Dan Rathers. I mean, I've seen a lot of them in the twenty-five years that I've been doing this. What was appealing about Oprah was that she came across as very much her own person. It was just that good. It was like, 'Wow! Here's the job! You want it?' "

Chris explains that a market like Nashville looks for different qualities in an anchorperson than perhaps a city such as New York or Chicago does. "This is a very laid-back market. We look for people who are authoritative in a friendly kind of way, not in a threatening or intimidating way. Not the voice from the mountain, but your next-door neighbor who knows what's going on and can tell you about it. That's what Oprah projected. She was somebody you'd like to have living next door to you who could tell you what was happening in town that day. She was very pleasant to take. She was very nice looking. She sounded great. She came across like she knew what she was saying."

After judging Oprah's audition tape, Chris had a conversation with WTV's general manager, Harold Crump, who ultimately made the decision to hire Oprah. Before accepting the job offered to her, however, Oprah first discussed it with Dr. Cox.

"She was on her way to biology class and got that call from Chris Clark, over at Channel 5," recalls Dr. Cox.

Oprah told Dr. Cox, "I have a chance to go on television."

"Well, what do you want me to do about it?" asked Dr. Cox.

"I need you to help me make a decision," said Oprah. "Should I give up school and radio?"

Dr. Cox was astonished that Oprah would even ask such a question. "I called her a few names," he says. "I told her what a fool she was to come to me. The fact that she was in college meant she should be able to make a decision like that, one that would affect her future, without my talk. She swears that I gave her a dime to make the call saying she would accept the job." Laughing, Dr. Cox adds, "By the way, she has never paid back my dime."

Referring to Chris Clark's job offer to Oprah, John Heidelberg says, "That kind of talent you swallow up quick. You don't let it get away."

"You know, you look for people all the time," says Chris Clark, "and everybody you see on tape, there's always this nagging doubt. Well, she's okay, but her hair's not right. Her makeup's not right. Why didn't she dress better?" With Oprah's tape, he says, there weren't any doubts. "It was unbelievable. You looked at Oprah the first time and you said, 'This is right. This will work.' It was just one of those things you don't experience very often."

Chris says that when WTV made the decision to hire Oprah the station broke ground on two levels. "She was hired to be the first female co-anchor in Nashville. She was also the first black co-anchor."

Unlike her first few weeks at WVOL, Oprah didn't go through a training period at WTV. Since she would be working on the weekend news, however, with a small staff, she was required to write her own script, which was new for her. "She had to learn how to do scripts," says Chris, "all the mechanical stuff, how we get things ready for the newscast and how we do them."

Oprah was teamed with Harry Chapman, who says working with a co-anchor for the first time was different. "Obviously it was something you had to get used to. Who's going to get what story? Who's gonna do the lead? At that time, we were also our own producers. We didn't have a weekend news producer. It was up to us. We put it together. We wrote it. We did the lineup (deciding the order of the stories). We did it all. It was our responsibility."

Chapman says a typical weekend news day shift would begin shortly after noon. The first thing he and Oprah would do was see the assignment editor, who had arrived earlier in the day to decide what stories would be covered and who would do them. In addition to anchoring, producing, and writing their own program, they also performed as reporters. When covering a story, they would be accompanied by a cameraman. "If it was a press conference, or if it was a shooting, we were out covering those stories just like reporters would," says Chapman. "We would come back and do the writing and the anchoring of it."

Recalling Oprah's work as a weekend reporter, Chapman says, "Oprah was the kind of person who really got involved. She was real close to whatever she was doing and had a lot of sympathy and empathy for those people that she was talking to."

When they returned to the station, Oprah and Chapman would work on writing their scripts while their film was being developed. "When it got to writing time we'd all sit down and write the news," Chapman says. "We'd determine what went where. We'd check the network to see what stories were available to us from there and write around those stories."

Chapman says he enjoyed working with Oprah. "It was

a good, comfortable working relationship. She was eager to pull her own load and do whatever any of the rest of us would do. She was willing to do anything and everything that needed to be done. That impressed me more than anything. Some people just don't have that willingness. But Oprah was eager to learn."

With less than six hours from the time they first walked through the station's doors, Oprah and Chapman would have to have everything ready for the six o'clock newscast. "After that newscast," says Chapman, "we would immediately sit down and start writing for the ten o'clock newscast. You'd grab a hamburger or something, for dinner, but generally you would start writing and rewriting stories for the ten o'clock newscast."

Recalling Oprah's on-air performance, Chapman says, "She was a natural, completely at ease in front of the camera. She was the kind of person who, if she messed up, would laugh at herself. She had a voice that was unlike anything else in the South. Southerners, whether they be white or black, tend to have a dialect and a whole different sound from the rest of the country. With Oprah, there was nothing of that. I guess that was probably a little bit of her growing up in the Midwest. She had a great gift."

"Even though she was the first female and the first black anchorperson," says Chris Clark, "I can recall only one negative call. And it was from a crank. We kept track of the calls. That's the only one I can recall, which speaks well as to how she was accepted by everybody."

"She was the thing over there," says John Heidelberg. "People were a little hesitant at first. But she won them over."

Although Oprah's résumé and professional biography, as well as a number of newspaper articles, have stated that she graduated from Tennessee State University with a B.A. degree in speech and performing arts, it wasn't until 1987 that Oprah actually received her degree. Her hectic schedule at WTV prevented her from completing her senior class project. Dr. Cox says, "That was the only thing preventing her from getting her degree." Dr. Williams jokes that she waited patiently for Oprah to submit her project so she could finally retire from TSU.

Within no time at all Oprah was quickly moved up to co-anchoring the weeknight news, a clear demonstration on management's part of its belief in her ability to attract ratings and, consequently, revenue for the station. WTV, a CBS affiliate, receives a substantial fee from the network for broadcasting its programing. The bulk of the money a station earns, however, is usually made from its local newscasts, where it is able to set its own advertising rates for commercials.

"She had a knack for deviating from the script," recalls Chris Clark. "If she was reading a sentence and it was just instinctively better to use different words she would use them. It wasn't planned that way. She made them sound more conversational. It would sound great."

"Most people were delighted we had on Channel 5 a black person who was a co-anchorperson," says Dr. Williams, who understood the challenge Oprah faced starting at WTV with virtually no training in television. "When Oprah was at TSU we didn't have any television and radio courses in our curriculum," she explains. "The emphasis then was in speech, communication, and theater." A sequence in television and radio was incorporated into the department shortly after Oprah left. "I wish while she was here we had then what we have now," Dr. Williams adds.

Even after Oprah left TSU to work at WTV, their paths still crossed frequently. Dr. Williams recalls, "She went around the community and covered various kinds of activities, such as the Black Expo, which gave her some kind of visibility."

Dr. Williams says Oprah even covered a story for WTV in her home. At the time, Dr. Williams's mother and her husband's mother, who were both in their eighties, were living with them. Speaking of her mother and mother-in-law, Dr. Williams says, "Oprah knew them when she was living here. She did a piece for Channel 5 on elderly people and came out to interview the mothers. I was impressed with the gentleness with which she handled them."

"I know that what you see is what she is," says Harry Chapman. "There's no faking about that. She is as she appears. I like her and respect her for that."

"You can tell who's faking it," adds Chris Clark. "Her emotions came right out there. That's what made her so good."

"You really can't afford to be anything else but be yourself, after all," Oprah explains. "Even if people don't like the subject or are not particularly interested in the subject, if you just always remain yourself or are able to tap into whatever it is about yourself that you can allow to be seen on camera, it works so much better."

"We tried to make her a reporter," recalls Chris Clark. "But that just didn't work out. She's too soft-hearted. She just couldn't do it. I'd send her out to cover a story on a family that had just been burned out. She would give them money out of her pocket and cry half the day over this situation. She would take it personally."

"I really agonized," confided Oprah to Judy Markey of *Cosmopolitan*. "I was a horrible writer, and I just broke down and cried with all those crime and fire stories. But I stuck it out, because I figured one day it could lead to a talk show."

In desperation, Chris Clark decided to send her out to the airport to interview a Turkish student. "There was some crisis in Turkey," he recalls. "I forget what it was, some crisis with Greece, or whatever. It was a big deal in Turkey. Anyway, we had a Turkish student coming in to study at Vanderbilt." He figured this was his last shot at making Oprah a reporter, win or lose. Playing Lou Grant to Oprah's Billie Newman, Chris Clark says, "I gave her my 'There's no small stories, only small reporters' speech. 'Every person has a story to tell.' I told Oprah, 'Go out to the airport and interview this person. Come back for the late news with your big story and we'll tie it in with the national story.'

"Well, she went out there. And this was in the days of film, before videotape. I think they had only given her eight minutes of film. She got out there and this student couldn't understand English very well. She kept asking the same question over and over for eight minutes. Finally, she turned to the camera and said, 'I give up!' The poor guy said, 'I'm sorry, I'm sorry.' Oprah touched him and said, 'It's all right. It's not your fault.'

"It's really a cute piece of film," says Chris Clark, adding that it's still shown at WTV parties. "She gave it her best shot, though."

Referring to Oprah's tendency to touch or hug people, particularly on her talk show, Chris Clark says, "That's very much Oprah. That's not calculated to be a trademark of hers. If she were talking to you she would want to touch you, have some kind of contact with you. It's a form of personal communication. Some people are aloof. They don't want to be that close to you. I'm sure she didn't realize she was doing it. But she does."

Chris Clark also remembers that he and his wife, Gloria, went to see Oprah perform once. "It was a one-woman show. She just stood on stage and talked about her life. It was just great. I told her afterward, 'You ought to be acting and not being an anchorperson.' We laughed about it then."

Oprah has told reporters that she understood one of the reasons WTV hired her was because they needed to fill a quota. "I was a token," she says. "But I was a happy, paid token."

Appearing as a panelist at the Middle Tennessee steering committee of International Women's Year in 1975, a year and a half after she had been hired to work at WTV, Oprah said, "I asked Chris Clark if he hired me because I was black and a woman. He answered, 'No, I hired you because you were a reporter, but I did need a black reporter.' "

Oprah recalled that one of the first stories she had reported for WTV took her to a segregated section of Nashville. Introduced to a shop owner, Oprah began to shake his hand when he said, "We don't shake hands with niggers down here." Oprah responded, "I'll bet the niggers are glad."

On the same panel, Oprah also said, "My basic concern with WTV is the quality of news coverage. We do too many things that do not warrant prime time. I talk with them about this as well as what we are doing for women and black women. They tell me that they are concerned and that it is an equal opportunity company."

Oprah pointed out that, at that time, there was one woman in management and that she was in an office position.

"The station does not feel that Nashville is ready for a woman as an anchorperson on a news program. They don't feel a woman can carry it alone. Unless pressure is exerted, things will remain the same," said Oprah.

A year later Oprah decided to leave WTV. Big changes were taking place in TV news where women were concerned. Barbara Walters had just left her position as co-host of NBC's "The Today Show" to become the first woman co-anchor of a weeknight network TV news program on ABC. She had signed a contract for one million dollars a year to co-anchor the evening news with Harry Reasoner. Ironically, at the time, other news anchors, mostly men, criticized the high salary ABC was paying Barbara Walters. Walter Cronkite, in particular, commented that he couldn't see the justification for paying that much money to anyone to anchor the news. But ABC-TV's successful bid for Barbara Walters set a trend in network TV news salaries that didn't come to a halt until the late eighties, when serious financial setbacks at all three networks initiated a reevaluation of the salaries paid to anchorpersons. In 1987, twelve years after Oprah's panel appearance, Barbara Walters remains the only woman to have regularly anchored a weeknight network news program, and even then she was a co-anchor. Nor has there been a single black anchorperson on a weeknight network news program.

When it was reported in *The Nashville Banner* that Oprah was leaving WTV to accept a position as co-anchorperson and reporter at WJZ-TV in Baltimore, Chris Clark told *The Nashville Banner*, "She is a tremendously talented person. We hate to lose her."

Recalling Oprah's decision to resign, Chris Clark says, "I was sick! Are you kidding? I was convinced that she was making the wrong move. She was on her way to being the leading anchor in this town in no time flat. She damn near was when she left."

Oprah's reasons for leaving Nashville to move to Baltimore weren't strictly professional. Although she was earning approximately fifteen thousand dollars a year as a leading anchor in Nashville, she was still expected to follow the rules set down by Vernon in his home. For instance, she still had a midnight curfew. Oprah was anxious to experience total independence. Relocating to Baltimore for a higher salary and a more prominent position in a bigger market seemed like the right incentives for making the move. She realized she was taking a risk, but understood her decision to leave Nashville wasn't irreversible. She would always be welcomed back into her father's home. WTV had also made it clear to Oprah she could have her job back without hesitation.

"She knew the door was open to come back," says Chris Clark, referring to a statement the station manager had made to Oprah. "But she was in the big time now."

7

What's an Oprah?

"They sent me to this chichi, pooh-pooh salon. And in a week I was bald. Just devastated. I had a French perm and it all fell out. Every little strand. I was left with three little squiggles in the front. They tried to change me, and then they're stuck with a bald, black anchorwoman."

Imagine a twenty-two-year-old, unknown black woman stepping in to co-anchor a new one-hour format of the "CBS Evening News" with Walter Cronkite at the height of his success and you'll understand the pressure Oprah faced when she arrived in Baltimore.

A Westinghouse executive had been following Oprah's work at WTV for seven months before offering her a position at WJZ-TV. Besides Barbara Walters's high salary and co-anchor position, which was expected to turn the tide on the national TV news scene, several changes were also taking place at local TV news operations. Most notably, news programs were being expanded from thirty minutes to an hour in many markets as a way of earning higher revenues. WJZ, which had the highest-rated evening newscast in Baltimore, was a forerunner in making the switch. WJZ station executives had hoped a one-hour local news program, with Oprah as part of the team, would keep viewers from switching to the CBS affiliate on the half hour to watch Walter Cronkite with his national news.

Expanding the news to an hour was just one of the many changes local stations, such as WJZ, had made in their format since the early seventies. Just like in Nashville, where Oprah had co-anchored the news with a white male, stations across the country, particularly in the bigger markets, such as New York and Chicago, were teaming their white anchormen with blacks, women, and other nontraditional on-camera personalities. Videotape had also replaced film as the leading format in presenting late-breaking, on-location news stories. This change, in fact, revolutionized the way news was presented. "You could shoot a city council meeting at ten till six and have it on the air at six o'clock," says Harry Chapman, Oprah's co-anchor in Nashville. "You couldn't do that with film. You didn't have to wait on that thirty to forty minutes in the soup [when the film is being developed] to get your video ready for a newscast. That was the magic of tape. We all thought it was wonderful. The immediacy was the big benefit."

WJZ, an ABC affiliate, had little reason to doubt that Baltimore's first one-hour newscast would be a success. High-rated programs such as "Happy Days" and "Laverne and Shirley," which had helped to make ABC-TV No. 1 in prime time for the first time in the network's history, provided WJZ with a huge audience to promote its one-hour news program. Station executives had designated Oprah to team with Jerry Turner, who, incidentally, is to Baltimore what Walter Cronkite was to America when he was still anchoring "CBS News." As a way to increase the number of stories presented on the news, four new reporters were added to the staff. WJZ's likable and extremely popular weatherman, Bob Turk, was slotted to deliver his weather report at 6:29 P.M., one full minute before Walter Cronkite began his news report.

In an effort to familiarize Oprah with Baltimore, station executives assigned her to head a forty-five-part series reporting on the city's diverse neighborhoods. The idea was conceived by a mayoral aide and presented to WJZ as a public relations move to promote Baltimore's annual city fair. After beginning work on the series, Oprah told a *Baltimore Evening Sun* reporter, "It was a great way of introducing me to the city. I probably know more about neighborhoods now than anybody else . . . at the station, I mean."

Discussing her interviewing technique, Oprah told the reporter she found that community association leaders did not make good interviewees. Instead, she'd get somebody on a street corner or in the corner drugstore to talk to her. Oprah added that she did minimal research for the series, depending instead on a "synopsis" of each neighborhood provided by the city. On the air, however, Oprah was credited with gathering the information for the series.

When asked how he felt about sharing anchor duties with Oprah, Jerry Turner told Bill Carter of *The Baltimore Sun*, "Oprah and I get along great. She's a great gal. I think many decisions in television are based on market research and apparently the research shows that one hour is too long a time for any one person to be on. I know I could do it. But I'm certainly not jealous."

Gary Elion, then the news director at WJZ, told Bill Carter he didn't think it was possible to team anyone with Jerry Turner who would threaten him. He also maintained that, in the Baltimore market, Turner was more popular than even Walter Cronkite. He believed that Turner would remain the city's No. 1 anchorperson. And it was made clear that Turner, and not Oprah, would open with the lead news story of the day.

Being teamed with Baltimore's heavyweight anchorman

in a new one-hour format wasn't Oprah's only problem. Some media critics blasted WJZ's decision to team Turner with an out-of-towner, especially one as young as Oprah, when the station already had what was considered another first-rate TV newsman working for it named Al Sanders. Since Sanders was pulling in the highest-rated news show in Baltimore on Sunday nights, why wasn't he teamed with Turner to launch the new one-hour format, they asked?

"Oprah walked into a tremendous position," recalls Bill Carter, TV critic for *The Baltimore Sun*. "WJZ's management had an idea that she had great things in her, that they really gave her a plum job." To herald Oprah's arrival in Baltimore, WJZ plastered billboards all over town asking the provocative question: "What's an Oprah?"

The pressure Oprah experienced at WJZ wasn't all that was troubling her. She admitted she was also having difficulty adjusting to Baltimore. Freed from the restraints of a midnight curfew, Oprah made it a point shortly after arriving in Baltimore to celebrate until dawn at a WJZ staff party. She was also hoping for something magical to happen, such as possibly meeting Mr. Right. "Unfortunately, as Doris Day used to say, nothing happened."

"It took me a year to become charmed by Baltimore," Oprah told a *News American* reporter. "The first time I saw the downtown area I got so depressed that I called my daddy in Nashville and burst into tears. In Nashville you had a yard even if you didn't have a porch. But the houses on Pennsylvania Avenue had neither."

Although Oprah had arrived in Baltimore in June 1976, the one-hour news show was postponed twice. Technical difficulties and an unprepared staff were the reasons cited by station management. Finally, on August 16, 1976, exactly one year before Elvis Presley's death, WJZ's one-hour news show premiered. In the presence of veteran newsman Turner, Oprah appeared stiff and intimidated.

When it became apparent to WJZ's management that

there were problems with the Oprah and Turner anchor team, Oprah immediately began feeling heat. All of a sudden, "What's an Oprah?" became, "What's right with Oprah?"

Things that had worked for Oprah in Nashville were considered out of place and inappropriate at WJZ. Oprah says her habit of never reading a script before airtime was criticized by WJZ's management. "I wanted to know the news at the same time everybody else did," she told *USA Today*. "By the time I got on the air, I'd be bored with it. And, boy, I got in a whole lot of trouble over that."

"The big time isn't all it's cracked up to be," says Chris Clark, referring to Oprah's move to Baltimore and the subsequent difficulties she encountered. "When she got to Baltimore and started having these problems, I just knew that was a mistake. These big markets will do things like that to you. It was a very sad time for her."

Nine months after the one-hour news show had premiered, on April Fool's Day, Oprah was told she was being relieved of her evening anchor duties. She was being replaced by Al Sanders, and she was being switched to early-morning cut-ins during ABC-TV's "Good Morning America." She was also assigned to work with WJZ's Instant Eye unit as a reporter for the 6 P.M. and 11 P.M. newscasts. Stephen Kimatian, WJZ's general manager, told Bill Carter of *The Baltimore Sun*, "We believe this is an opportunity for her to develop herself, to work more on her own. When people see how Oprah does on the assignments she is given they will be convinced that the profile we have of Oprah is a high one."

It was reported that Oprah took the news gracefully. Gary Elion, who was now departing as news director of WJZ, told Bill Carter, "I think she understands it. I think she sees this as an opportunity to stand on her own as Oprah, not as a partner to a giant like Jerry Turner."

Oprah, meanwhile, viewed the switch, understand-

Oprah and her high-school boyfriend, Anthony Otey, were voted
Most Popular Girl and Most Popular Boy at Nashville's East
High School. (Courtesy Anthony Otey)

"**O**prah was somebody you'd like to have living next door to you, who could tell you what was happening in town that day," says Chris Clark, Oprah's first television boss. Above is an early shot of Oprah from that first job. (Courtesy WTVF, Nashville)

Pictured here is Oprah at work at her first television job at WTVF, Nashville. Oprah once revealed to her audience, "When I did my first audition for my first television job, I was such a nervous wreck I had no idea what to do or say. And I thought, maybe I'll just pretend I'm Barbara Walters." Hearing Oprah's story, Barbara Walters told Oprah, "Thank goodness you got the job!" (Courtesy WTVF, Nashville)

"My dad really held me in with a tight rein," says Oprah of Vernon Winfrey, above. "Without his direction, I'd have wound up pregnant and another statistic." (*The Nashville Banner*)

"I get concerned that no one knows about Oprah's experience here in theater. Most people get the idea that her first major acting move was in *The Color Purple*," remarks Dr. William Cox, one of Oprah's favorite drama teachers at Tennessee State University. (Courtesy Dr. William Cox)

"There were times when she was a little despondent," says John Heidelberg, Oprah's first radio boss. In fact, criticism from some station employees caused Oprah to doubt her own talent. (Courtesy John Heidelberg)

Oprah's first TV boss, Chris Clark, said he could only recall one negative comment during Oprah's tenure as Nashville's first black female television anchorperson. "And it was from a crank," observed Clark. (Courtesy WTVF, Nashville)

"**S**ome people don't know how to take me sometimes, but I'm honest. I really am. I just say what I feel and hope it works."
(Don Fisher © 1985)

One way Oprah spends her reported thirty-one-million-dollar salary is by providing a full scholarship for kids like Chris Gardner, a student at The Chicago Academy of Performing Arts. (Carl Sissac)

Oprah enjoys socializing with America's most prominent politicians, such as Chicago's late Mayor Harold Washington. (Carl Sissac)

Oprah and her predecessor, former "A.M. Chicago" host Robb Weller, share a smile at a Chicago charity function. (Carl Sissac)

Before meeting former model Stedman Graham, Oprah was convinced she'd never be involved in another relationship. "We have our problems," acknowledges Stedman. "You just have to be grounded. You have to know where you're going and block out the B.S." (Carl Sissac)

When *The Color Purple's* producer Quincy Jones caught a glimpse of Oprah on her talk show, he exclaimed, "That's Sofia!" (AP/Wide World Photos)

"It was the one time in my life I experienced total harmony," says Oprah of her work in *The Color Purple*. (AP/Wide World Photos)

Pictured above are the five nominees for Best Supporting Actress in the 1985 Oscars competition. Front, left to right, are Meg Tilly (*Agnes of God*) and Margaret Avery (*The Color Purple*); back, left to right, are Amy Madigan (*Twice in a Lifetime*), Angelica Huston (*Prizzi's Honor*), and Oprah. (AP/Wide World Photos)

At a press conference held to announce syndication of "The Oprah Winfrey Show," Oprah is joined by chairman of King World Productions Roger King. (AP/Wide World Photos)

Considering the debris on Oprah's desk, it's no wonder she admits, "My friends say I need to be more organized." (AP/Wide World Photos)

Oprah's innate sense of what viewers want to see brought her to Forsyth County, Georgia, where no blacks had lived for more than fifty years. Her broadcasts put her on the front pages of newspapers across America. (AP/Wide World Photos)

Oprah donned a purple-dyed fur for the New York premiere of *The Color Purple*. (Gamma Liaison/ Judy Sloan)

Oprah attributes her slimmer figure at the 1986 Oscars ceremony to drinking lots of water, as well as a two-week stay at the Rancho la Puerta Health Spa in Mexico. Between the spa and her gown (designed by Bob Mackie), Oprah spent an estimated $10,000. (Gamma Liaison/Laura Luongo)

Before appearing on Oprah's show, Christie Brinkley feared that Oprah might be brutal. After the interview, however, Christie confided to friends, "I had a better feeling from that interview than any I've done!" (Don Fisher © 1985)

"I'd never been around a group of working women and been on a show like this where it was so comfortable for me to be on," said Candice Bergen after her appearance on Oprah's talk show. (Don Fisher © 1985)

One reason Oprah is able to get guests such as Brooke Shields to open up on her show is because she's been so open about her own life. "Oprah's had such an incredible life that no matter what topic we do, it usually happened to her," says producer Debbie DeMaio. (Don Fisher © 1985)

One of the qualities Shirley MacLaine admires in Oprah is her confidence. "You knew Oprah Winfrey believed in herself and she wasn't going to have an iota of doubt or fear," said Shirley. (Don Fisher © 1985)

When Whoopie Goldberg married in 1986, she left her little black book to Oprah. Reading it, Oprah was surprised to find that it included such well-known names as Bruce Willis, Don Johnson, and Warren Beatty. (Fineman/Sygma)

"I allow myself to be vulnerable. It's not something I consciously do. But I am. It just happens that way. I'm vulnerable, and people say, 'Poor thing. She has big hips, too.'" (Courtesy King World Productions)

"I am those women," says Oprah, speaking of her viewers. "I am everyone of them. And they are me. That's why we get along so well." (Courtesy King World Productions)

"I never think about what I'm going to ask. Ever! The red light comes on and I say, 'Well, something has to happen here!'" (Courtesy King World Productions)

ably, as a demotion. She felt that, here she was, twenty-two years old, a little green, and anchoring the six o'clock news in a major market. Despite the bad chemistry between her and Jerry Turner, an optimistic Oprah had mistakenly believed that all that was required of her was to go on the air and do the best she could. She later told the *News American*, "I think the real reason we weren't a good match was because I needed to do a lot of growing. I was twenty-two when I came here and sitting down with the god of local anchormen intimidated me."

With Gary Elion gone from WJZ, the assistant news director decided it was time to begin correcting some of Oprah's "faults." She later told Mike Wallace of "60 Minutes," "The assistant news director came to me and said, 'Your hair's too long. It's too thick. Your eyes are too far apart. Your nose is too wide. Your chin is too wide. And you need to do something about it.' You thought Christine Craft [an anchorwoman who was fired because her bosses didn't think viewers found her attractive] had problems.

"They sent me to this chichi, pooh-pooh salon. And in a week I was bald. Just devastated. I had a French perm and it all fell out. Every little strand. I was left with three little squiggles in the front. They tried to change me, and then they're stuck with a bald, black anchorwoman. I went through a real period of self-discovery. You have to find other reasons for appreciating yourself. It's certainly not your looks."

Oprah decided to cover her baldness with a wig, but quickly discovered yet another problem. She told *Good Housekeeping*, "There were no wigs big enough for my head—it's twenty-four inches around—so I had to walk around wearing scarves for several months."

Fortunately, a bright spot in the whole ugly mess was that Oprah was dating a man who was there to give moral support when she needed it. His name was Lloyd Kramer and he also worked as a reporter in Baltimore. After losing her hair, Oprah was touched to discover that Lloyd actually valued her for who she was and not what she was. She joked that he loved her even when she was bald and added that he was one of the most fun romances she had ever experienced.

The assistant news director also found problems with Oprah's speaking style and she was quickly hustled off to a speech coach in New York to correct it. The speech coach told Oprah she was never going to succeed in broadcasting unless she first toughened up. She accused Oprah of being too nice. This totally confused Oprah. She *wanted* people to think she was nice. Even after her Chicago success Oprah said, "I think probably the biggest problem in raising me was I was raised to be a nice girl. My biggest, biggest fault right now is that I do not express anger very well. And I certainly want to be liked by as many people as I possibly can, which gets me in a lot of trouble. I avoid confrontation at all costs." She could just as easily have been speaking of her early experiences in Baltimore.

Sent out to cover tragedies, Oprah found the assignments increasingly more difficult to handle. She cringed when she was sent out to interview a distraught woman who had just lost her children and house in a tragic fire. Oprah's bosses wanted her to find out how the woman felt about her loss. At first Oprah refused to do it, but she was told to cover the story or lose her job. Oprah carried through on the assignment. After reporting it live, however, she apologized to the woman and her audience for having done the interview. Speaking of other stories she was assigned to cover as a reporter, Oprah recalls, "You're at a plane crash and you're standing right there and you're smelling the charred bodies, and people are coming to find out if their relatives are in the crash and they're weeping, and you weep too because it's a tragic thing."

Comparing Oprah's tenure at WTV to the experience she faced covering the news in Baltimore, Chris Clark said, "You had to let Oprah be Oprah. I don't think we made the first suggestion as to how she should wear her hair, or what she should dress in. I don't think we did that. We just had to let Oprah do her thing. That's the only way it ever really works out. You can't change people. In television what you see is what you get. We saw that with Oprah. Why do it? It was working and it was Oprah."

In the television business, employees come to expect overnight reversals. As the ink is drying on a multi-year million-dollar contract, a Phyllis George can be told she's out of work. An actor's promised that his new series is a definite go and then discovers, hours before its scheduled premiere, that the show has already been canceled. You can be co-anchoring the six o'clock news one day and be out on the street the next working as a roving reporter in search of a story. If you're resilient, you stick it out, understanding everything can change again. Sometimes you can even leave the studio, bidding good night to one station manager, and arrive at work the following morning only to hear, "Welcome aboard!" from a new one. For Oprah, the topsy-turvy changes taking place at WJZ were finally about to turn in her favor.

8

"People Are Talking"

"People think because I'm in television I have this great social life. Let me tell you, I can count on my fingers the number of dates I've had in the four years I've been in Baltimore, and that includes the ones I paid for."

"**W**hen I was doing television in Nashville, I was given a stand-in job for just one day filling in on one of those local talk-show community-affairs programs that air at two in the morning. I remember being given the opportunity, just on a temporary basis, and thinking this is what I'd like to do."

In the spring of 1977, a new station manager arrived at WJZ-TV from another Group W station in Cleveland and decided to shake things up. One of his first major moves was to develop a daily morning talk show to compete with "Donahue," which had become extremely popular in Baltimore. He decided that the best way would be to make the talk show something that would appeal to the people of

Baltimore and reflect their interests. Although Oprah was working as a reporter, the new station manager picked her to co-host the new show, which would be called "People Are Talking." "He immediately decided Oprah was a potential star," recalls Bill Carter.

Oprah, however, didn't share the new station manager's vision about "People Are Talking." She viewed her new position as primarily a demotion, a device to ease her out of news, and eventually out of WJZ-TV.

Richard Sher, a native of Baltimore, was tapped to co-host "People Are Talking" with Oprah. Sher had extensive broadcasting experience, in front of the camera as well as behind the scenes.

Bill Carter recalls that the premiere of "People Are Talking" was preceded by a heavy promotional blitz. To insure a high rating, the first show's scheduled guests were actors from the ABC-TV daytime soap "All My Children," which was extremely popular in Baltimore. Reviewing the premiere show, Bill Carter was disappointed. "I remember thinking they had picked such a ridiculous, typical kind of guest. How could they be planning to do anything original? It wasn't what it was built up to be."

Oprah had a different reaction to the premiere show. "I came off the air, and I knew that was what I was supposed to do. It just felt like breathing. It was the most natural process for me."

Teaming Oprah with Richard Sher clicked with viewers. "The show become successful rather quickly," says Bill Carter.

When Richard Sher later appeared on Oprah's national show, they discussed their working relationship. Because there were two hosts, there were times when both wanted to ask a question at the same time. As a way of dealing with the situation, they developed a special form of communication. "We tapped each other," Oprah explained.

"Sometimes we overtapped each other," said Richard

Sher. "When Oprah wanted to ask a question, she would tap me. But if I thought I had a better question, I would tap her. The audience had no idea what we were doing."

During the height of "People Are Talking's" popularity, a local Baltimore community newspaper interviewed Oprah and Richard Sher and wanted to know if they ever argued. "If I don't like something Richard's doing, I tell him," answered Oprah.

"We've never had a major fight," added Richard Sher. "I don't talk behind her back—there's a lot of that going on in this business—and she knows exactly where I'm coming from."

"Put it this way," Oprah volunteered, "sometimes he can be difficult. But I understand a lot."

Dick Maurice, entertainment editor of *The Las Vegas Sun*'s showbiz section, was a guest on "People Are Talking" when Oprah was co-host and described her as "one of the most sincere people that you would ever want to talk to." His reaction to Richard Sher, however, was less than favorable. "He was very much into himself," explains Dick Maurice. "When he would ask you a question, and the camera was on you, he would turn to people on the side and mimic to them to get him coffee or whatever. Here's a guy who asks you a question, and then he doesn't even listen to the answer.

"Oprah would pick it up and save it."

Since Dick Maurice covers the entertainment beat, he's constantly asked personal questions about celebrities. He recalls that when he arrived one morning to make an appearance on "People Are Talking," Richard Sher asked him which Hollywood celebrities were gay. He says Richard Sher's next question was, "Are you gay?" Dick Maurice was stunned by the question because it "came out of left field."

Fortunately, Oprah managed to smooth things over. "She just jumped in and saved what could've been a heated argument."

Dick continues, "She used to come into the makeup room,

like a little girl, and sit down on a stool while I was being made up and ask questions about people she was interested in. She had this quest for information about stars. Yet, it was not vicious and evil. You know, 'I want the latest gossip. Gimme the dirt.'

"You enjoyed gossiping with her. She'd never come on the show and use the information. She was the kind of person you'd like to spend time with.

"One time we were talking about my dad. When he was eighteen years old he lost his face in the war in Normandy. Because of the fact that he was so disfigured, he would never go with me to father-and-son banquets, things like that. I was telling her how kids would call me the son of Frankenstein and how my father used to drop me off two blocks from school, rather than bear the embarrassment. I was sitting there in the makeup room, being made up, and I looked over and tears were coming down her face. She was sitting there crying as I was telling the story.

"She had a special quality about her that made her unique. There was this way she had of looking at you, and you felt that, when you were talking to her, the only person she was thinking about was you. It was a look in her eyes. You could see a soul there."

Although Oprah was finally enjoying success in Baltimore as co-host of "People Are Talking," her love life took a turn for the worse. Her steady boyfriend, Lloyd Kramer, announced that he had accepted a job offer at a New York TV station. Oprah's way of coping with the loss was to turn to food. "I would hear stories about how she would have binges of eating when she was lonely," says Bill Carter.

Because she's so open about her feelings, Oprah began to present herself as a lonely woman. She told the *News American*, "People think because I'm in television I have this great social life. Let me tell you, I can count on my fingers the number of dates I've had in the four years I've been in Baltimore, and that includes the ones I paid for."

"She would joke about it on the air," recalls Bill Carter. "To people at the station she would definitely say that she had no social life."

Like so many people who find themselves lonely and insecure, Oprah became her own worst enemy. Overeating was only one of the ways she sabotaged her own happiness. As a way of filling the day, she began taking on extra assignments at WJZ-TV. This would insure that she wouldn't have a social life, even if she could. Besides co-hosting "People Are Talking" every morning, Oprah also anchored the noon news report, as well as filming an occasional story, usually something with human-interest appeal, for the evening news. "That's a lot of work for anybody," says Bill Carter.

But not for Oprah. When WJZ-TV decided to go with an early local newscast, scheduled to air before ABC-TV's early morning newscast, Oprah volunteered to anchor it. "I remember, at the time, questioning why someone who was already doing so much, and was succeeding at so much, would want to take on yet another assignment, especially one that would force her to get up at some ridiculous hour," says Bill Carter. "The answer I got from an inside source at the station was that Oprah's social life was so muddled that she was looking to do this because it would give her an excuse not to have a social life. She'd have to go to bed early."

Oprah reportedly told people at the station, "I'm not doing anything at night, anyway. I might as well go to bed early."

"In retrospect," says Bill Carter, "it almost sounds beyond belief because she's so outgoing and social now."

Oprah has said she was involved seriously with only two men while she lived in Baltimore. After Lloyd Kramer moved to New York, she eventually became involved with a man she said her friends had warned her to stay away from. "I was a doormat," she says.

Oprah explains that the reason she allowed herself to be

badly treated was because, despite her professional success, she felt worthless without a man. Her second relationship was so rocky, she says, that she once missed three days of work because she didn't have the energy to get out of bed.

Things finally came to a head on September 8, 1981, when Oprah says she finally decided to commit suicide. She told Joan Barthel of *Ms.* magazine, "I don't think I was really serious about suicide, but I wrote my best friend a note." She said it was Saturday, around 8:30 P.M., and that she had been on the floor crying. In the letter she informed her best friend where she kept her insurance policies and other important documents. She also asked her to take care of her plants.

Oprah said that friends had urged her to seek counseling, but she felt she was too much her own person and couldn't do it.

Oprah said she had a personal revelation the night she had considered suicide. She told Joan Barthel, "I realized there was no difference between me and an abused woman who has to go to a shelter, except I could stay home. It was emotional abuse, which happens to women who stay in relationships that do not allow them to be all that they can be. You're not getting knocked around physically, but in terms of your ability to soar, your wings are clipped."

Armed with that self-revelation, Oprah said she began taking the first steps toward extricating herself from what was considered a destructive relationship.

Although *The Color Purple* was Oprah's film debut, many people don't know that she made her national acting debut on television. She was an "under-fiver," an actor who has less than five lines, on an episode of "All My Children" in 1983. When Agnes Nixon, the show's creator, had appeared on "People Are Talking," Oprah explained to her that she was a hard-core fan of the program. A short time later, Oprah was asked to make an appearance.

Oprah apparently firmly believed in the adage, "There are

no small parts, only small actors," because she approached her role with the enthusiasm of a leading lady tackling a Tennessee Williams play on Broadway. "I'm so blessed!" Oprah told Luther Young of *The Baltimore Sun.* "Imagine *me* doing this."

In preparation for her role, Oprah spent more than $1,200 buying three different outfits. She was scheduled to appear in one scene.

Luther Young accompanied Oprah to New York for her TV acting debut. He says that, en route to the studio, Oprah rehearsed her lines, much to the bewilderment of their cabdriver. "Excuse me," Oprah said, reciting a line from the script, "aren't you Pamela Kingsley?"

They arrived at the studio, on New York's Upper West Side, at 8 A.M. Since Oprah already had a strong background in theater training, she was curious about how the cast and crew of a daytime soap went about putting together a complete one-hour episode in one day.

The workday began with an early walk-through rehearsal. Next came a blocking rehearsal so that actors would know where to stand for the cameras. This was followed by a dress rehearsal and, finally, at 7 P.M. the episode was actually taped.

Since Oprah had only a few lines, and they were well-memorized, she used her time at the studio to introduce herself to each and every actor present for the day's taping. "I'm trying not to be excited," she confided to Luther Young. "I'm trying not to be star-struck."

Actress Kathleen Khami, who played Pamela Kingsley, recalls Oprah's day on the set of "All My Children." "She was incredibly energetic," says Kathleen. "And she was a big fan of the show."

Kathleen Khami says that when she went home that night she told her mother, "There was a talk-show host at the studio and she had this really strange name. Not bad strange, just different. We were trying to figure out where it came from."

Oprah also utilized her visit to observe the actors working on their scenes. "You could see that she was gonna get someplace," says Kathleen Khami. "She knew what she was doing. She was in her right environment. That was where she belonged."

Oprah's scene with Kathleen Khami took place in a restaurant named Nexus. "I can't believe I'm in Nexus without a date," Oprah said to Luther Young. "It's just like in Baltimore."

Besides Oprah and the principal actors, there were also a dozen extras seated at various tables throughout the restaurant. Oprah commented to Luther Young, "I always thought people in the background were just mumbling. These fools were actually asking me about the weather."

When the time came for Oprah's scene, she took her position at the assigned place. With the cameras rolling, she approached Kathleen Khami, who was seated at another table in the restaurant with an actor, and asked, "Excuse me, aren't you Pamela Kingsley?" As the producer watched Oprah's performance from the control booth she commented, "She's pretty good."

For her day's work Oprah was paid $183.75. She told Luther Young, "Someday I'd really love to do this. I'm just a show-biz kid."

With Oprah as co-host of "People Are Talking," the show became so successful that, at one point, reruns were even shown at night. Since "People Are Talking" was trouncing "Donahue" in the ratings, Group W, the broadcasting company that owned WJZ-TV, decided to team up with Program Syndication Services to try and syndicate the show nationally. As it turned out, Baltimore's version of "People Are Talking" was picked up by more than twelve cities, such as Sacramento and Milwaukee. "People Are Talking," however, was unable to achieve elsewhere the same kind of success it had experienced in Baltimore and was quietly pulled from syndication. Oprah was reportedly extremely disappointed.

After six successful years of hosting "People Are Talking," Oprah was growing restless. Although she liked Richard Sher and valued their friendship, she found she was beginning to feel cramped working with a partner. The few times that she had hosted "People Are Talking" solo, such as when Richard Sher was on vacation, Oprah sensed her own personal style emerging and it intrigued her.

"I had the feeling that she had her sights set on something else," says Dick Maurice. "I don't know whether she knew what she had in mind, but she was always asking about different markets. She'd bring up L.A. and ask, 'Who's the host out there?' Or she'd want to know how Regis Philbin was doing in New York. She knew all of the other markets. Any other talk-show host is usually not that knowledgeable about other talk shows."

"When you have finished growing in one place or time, you know. Your soul tells you when it's time to move on," Oprah says.

All she needed was incentive.

9
"A.M. Chicago"

"My first day in Chicago, September fourth, 1983, I set foot in this city, and just walking down the street, it was like roots, like the motherland. I knew I belonged here."

Before there was "A.M. Chicago," there was "Kennedy & Company," a popular morning TV talk show that occupied the time slot "Good Morning America" has held in Chicago since its premiere November 3, 1975, on ABC-TV's owned-and-operated station WLS-TV. Bob Kennedy, host of "Kennedy & Company," possessed a likable, good-natured personality and enjoyed interviewing non-celebrities, also known as regular people, as much as celebrities. His natural, fresh, down-to-earth personality endeared him to Chicago morning TV viewers.

"Kennedy & Company" worked without a studio audience, although calls were taken from viewers watching at home. Unlike Oprah's show, or "Donahue," where technology has made it possible for the caller's voice to materialize seemingly out of thin air, a telephone console was placed prominently on the set of "Kennedy & Company," in clear view of the TV viewing audience. Kennedy would say, "Let's take a call from someone at home," punch a button on the phone, and the caller would begin talking. In comparison to the advances that have been made in television since the early seventies, such as satellite broadcasting and cable TV, which enables a viewer to interact with his TV set, punching a button on a phone console to talk to a viewer watching at home seems quaint and somewhat primitive. Back in 1970, though, it seemed like a pretty amazing setup.

Immediately following "Kennedy & Company," "The Prize Movie" would begin airing with host Ionne, who also offered exercise tips and asked movie trivia questions. A viewer would call in with an answer, and if the answer was correct, the viewer would win whatever amount of money was in the show's featured jackpot. If, however, the caller was wrong, the amount of money in the jackpot increased until someone called with the correct answer. It was comfortable, local programming that didn't possess a hard-edge, cynical lust for viewers, which has since become standard for many locally produced TV talk shows in major markets.

In 1974, almost two years before "Good Morning America's" premiere, ABC-TV launched plans to develop a combination information and entertainment program that would compete with NBC-TV's popular "Today Show" for early morning viewers. The program was eventually titled "A.M. America." To distinguish "A.M. America" from the "Today Show," a concept was created to broadcast the show live from both the East Coast and the West Coast. Because of Bob Kennedy's popularity with viewers on Chicago's WLS-TV, ABC-TV executives tapped him to host the East Coast portion, with Ralph Story hosting from the West Coast. Peter Jennings was appointed to anchor the news segments. Ironically, when the "Today Show" premiered in 1952, NBC-TV turned to its Chicago station, WMAQ-TV, and hired

Dave Garroway, a popular local TV personality, to host the program.

With "A.M. America" scheduled to premiere in "Kennedy & Company's" time slot, WLS-TV bumped its "Prize Movie" for a newly created talk show titled "A.M. Chicago." The title was a gimmick other ABC-TV affiliates were also employing as a way to make their local talk shows seem compatible with "A.M. America." Steve Edwards, a Boston-based TV talk-show personality, was hired to host "A.M. Chicago." Appearing on Oprah's show in early 1987, Steve Edwards said, "I'm known as the guy who was the guy before the guy before Oprah." In simpler terms, he was "A.M. Chicago's" first host, Oprah was its third—the second host we'll get to later.

Shortly before the premiere of "A.M. America" in 1975, Bob Kennedy's doctor informed him he had cancer and that the condition was terminal. Bill Beutel, a New York anchorman, was hired to replace Kennedy on "A.M. America." Less than a year later, Chicago would be mourning the death of another prominent public figure, longtime Mayor Richard M. Daley, who suffered a fatal heart attack. Daley's death created changes so sweeping in Chicago that it inadvertently set the stage for Oprah's arrival as host of "A.M. Chicago" eight years later.

With Steve Edwards as host, "A.M. Chicago" managed to pull respectable ratings. Viewers found his warm, self-effacing style appealing and he was eventually accepted as a Chicago celebrity. Discussing TV talk-show hosts on Oprah's show later, Steve Edwards said, "We are strange people. We are all highly neurotic people. Otherwise, why would we want to put our faces on television every day and think that people want to hear whatever we have to say and ask? Fortunately, we live in a world where we get rewarded for it. But this is a strange group of people. All of us have interviewed Siamese twins. All of us have had animals poop on us. This is a strange category of people."

"A.M. America," however, wasn't as successful as "A.M. Chicago" in attracting viewers. The audience was confused by the former's constant switching from one coast to another and found it jarring. As a way of trying to improve the show, ABC-TV executives tinkered with its format and, in the process, succeeded only in making "A.M. America" seem even more inconsistent and unstable to viewers. Even more continuity was lost when Stefanie Edwards stepped down as co-host. To fill in the gap, celebrities such as Candice Bergen, Lynn Redgrave, and journalist Barbara Howar were signed to make temporary appearances as guest hosts. But before "A.M. America" reached its first anniversary, ABC-TV decided to cancel the show and replaced it with a completely revamped version retitled "Good Morning America," with David Hartman as host.

After three years of hosting "A.M. Chicago," Steve Edwards turned in his resignation. Anxious for network exposure, he relocated to Hollywood, where he hosted a popular locally produced program titled "Two on the Town." He was temporarily replaced by Charlie Rose, now host of CBS's "Nightwatch." Next, Robb Weller, who had been hosting a successful cable-TV talk show in Columbus, Ohio, took over. During Weller's stint as host of "A.M. Chicago," WBBM-TV, CBS-TV's Chicago station, acquired the rights to "Donahue" and slotted it directly against "A.M. Chicago." For a while, "A.M. Chicago" and "Donahue" ran neck-and-neck in the ratings, with Regis Philbin's short-lived morning talk show on NBC-TV, which featured Mary Hart as his co-host, pulling a disappointing third. "A.M. Chicago," with Robb Weller as host, also competed in 1980 against David Letterman's NBC-TV morning series. Letterman's morning show, which lasted less than six months, ran a poor third to "A.M. Chicago."

Like Steve Edwards, Robb Weller, after five years of hosting "A.M. Chicago," decided he was ready to try his luck elsewhere. "Donahue" had successfully become entrenched in first place in the Chicago market. In an attempt to lure viewers away from "Donahue," "A.M. Chicago" became increasingly dependent on actors from ABC-TV's top-rated daytime soaps as guests on the show. This bothered Weller, who felt "A.M. Chicago's" format was becoming boringly predictable. When it became apparent things weren't going to change, Weller decided not to renew his contract and signed on as host of WCBS's new series titled, coincidentally, "Two on the Town." By relocating to New York, Weller figured he'd have a better shot at being seen by network TV executives. New Yorkers, however, didn't share the same affection for its version of "Two on the Town" that Los Angeles viewers did and the show was quickly replaced by the syndicated "Wheel of Fortune," which became, of course, a huge success.

When Robb Weller quit as host of "A.M. Chicago" (eventually finding himself a successor to Steve Edwards again, now as co-host, with Mary Hart, of "Entertainment Tonight"), a replacement had not yet been found. Local WLS-TV personalities, such as news anchorpeople, and national celebrities, usually daytime soap opera actors, were used as guest hosts. This distressed Debbie DiMaio, "A.M. Chicago's" new young producer and former producer of "People Are Talking," who figured, "Great. Here, I've just walked away from a successful TV talk show in Baltimore to produce a third-rated one that now doesn't have a permanent host!" Then an inspired idea struck her. Fully aware that Oprah was restless in Baltimore, she called her and suggested she put together an audition reel, also known as a sample of her work, so that she could apply for the position as host of "A.M. Chicago." At the same time, unknown to Oprah, WLS-TV executives were already considering her potential as a replacement after having viewed her work on Debbie's audition reel. Oprah told *Ebony* her initial reaction to auditioning for hosting duties at "A.M. Chicago" was, "You can forget it. They're not going to put a black woman on at nine in the morning—not in Chicago, not on prime-time morning television."

Oprah's impression of Chicago, like that of most Americans, was shaped by recent reports on the network TV news, which portrayed it as a racially polarized city. Five months earlier, Chicago had elected its first black mayor, Harold Washington, whose victory was largely influenced by a heavy turnout of black voters. During the hotly contested campaign, Oprah recalled seeing a report on the network TV news where a young white student was asked whom he'd vote for as mayor and the boy responded that he'd vote for Bernard Epton, the white candidate. When asked why, the boy answered, "Because he's white."

Oprah's reluctance to audition as host of "A.M. Chicago" was also influenced by another emotion, sheer panic. She later said, "When Debbie left Baltimore to come here, and I got a call from WLS-TV saying, 'We'd like a tape,' I panicked. I just panicked. I didn't know what to do."

Oprah recalled that former colleagues in Baltimore had repeatedly asked, "Are you gonna be around here the rest of your life? You're really talented. When are you gonna put some tapes together?"

"Well," explained Oprah, "I'm the most disorganized person on earth, and maybe I'm not gonna get that accomplished in this lifetime. I'm tired of worrying about it."

She added, "I am the kind of person who—in all my years of television history—has not put one résumé or tape together. I always figured when it's time to go, somebody will call me." And that's exactly what was happening.

Oprah's inexperience in dealing with this situation, besides creating anxiety, also embarrassed her, particularly since being organized to look for work was something she had lectured about for years to students in Baltimore. "All these times I've talked to kids in schools, and said it was very important to have a résumé. It was very important to know what your skills are."

Being fortunate enough to have never had to actively seek employment, it was understandable that Oprah didn't know the first thing about putting together a résumé. "I thought, 'Oh my goodness! What am I going to say? What am I going to do?'" After giving the situation serious consideration, Oprah ended up doing what any sensible, intelligent person who could afford it would have done. "I went to a résumé expert."

With her résumé and audition reel in hand, Oprah arrived in Chicago to meet with WLS-TV's executives. She says, "I'll tell you this, my first day in Chicago, September fourth, 1983, I set foot in this city, and just walking down the street, it was like roots, like the motherland. I knew I belonged here."

Oprah later told Jon Anderson of *The Chicago Tribune* that before meeting with the WLS-TV executives she wanted to first watch an installment of "A.M. Chicago," which had already begun using guest hosts. She said, "I sat down in my hotel room and watched the show. I had never seen it before." Observing the show's format, as well as the guest host, Oprah added, "I thought, 'Listen! Not good! Too frivolous!'" Armed with knowledge of the show, Oprah gained confidence to share her own ideas about what would work on "A.M. Chicago." "I'm best at combinations—a sexual surrogate one day, Donny and Marie Osmond the next day, then the Klan."

Addressing the Chicago Broadcast Ad Club later, Oprah related her first meeting with WLS-TV's executives: "We were all sitting around the office and I said to Dennis [Swanson, WLS-TV's vice president and general manager], 'Well, you know I'm black.'

"He said, 'Yeah, yeah, I'm aware of that.'

"And I said, 'Ah, well, you know, I'm interested in whether you big executive types sat around and had any discussions about me being black, you know.'

"He said, 'Well, Oprah, let me tell you. I don't care what

color you are. You can be green. All we want to do is win. I'm in the business of winning and I want you to go for it.' "

Discussing WLS-TV's selection of Oprah as the new host of "A.M. Chicago," Dennis Swanson told Pamela Noel, "She was the best and we wanted the best."

To insure that a good deal was negotiated in her best interests, Oprah hired agent Ron Shapiro to represent her in talks with WLS-TV. Meanwhile, with negotiations under way, Oprah found herself turning to a familiar crutch for comfort, food. Finally, Shapiro reached an agreement with WLS-TV that was lucrative for both parties and Oprah signed a four-year contract for a salary reported at two hundred thousand dollars per year. After signing the contract, Oprah continued to overeat, this time to celebrate. She then discovered, to her dismay, that in six months she had gained twenty pounds.

WJZ-TV, like WTV-TV in Nashville seven years earlier, was horrified to discover Oprah would be leaving. Why, WJZ-TV executives asked Oprah, would she want to relocate to Chicago to compete with Donahue on his own turf, when she was already comfortably beating him in the ratings as co-host of "People Are Talking"? Before Oprah signed her contract with WLS-TV, WJZ-TV offered her a new contract, with a substantial increase in salary. In the end, however, WJZ-TV couldn't afford to match WLS-TV's offer.

"When she went to Chicago I did think she had a chance to succeed," says Bill Carter. "But a lot of other people didn't. There was an undercurrent of feeling here that this woman was not all that special. I guess because people are used to turning on their television sets and seeing nothing but attractive women, sexy or whatever. They really didn't see that substance in her. I think there's an element of racism in that. Oprah is a very black-looking black woman. Personally, I think she's very attractive. But it was that element. There were some people in this town who thought it was crazy for her to try to go out to

Chicago, that she could never succeed in that sort of more intense media atmosphere. I knew that was baloney because I had seen so many other people connecting with her. There were expectations that she would flop in Chicago."

Career reasons aside, Oprah had another motive, one that quite possibly was just as strong, for wanting to relocate to Chicago. It would finally bring an end to her stormy four-year relationship with a man who was unable to appreciate her personal worth. By making the first move, Oprah would be taking control of her personal life, as well as her professional one. She stood on the brink of no longer having to view herself as a woman who depended on a man for self-validation.

In a sense, it was a natural step for Oprah to take. When she left Nashville in 1976 she was a young woman of twenty-two seeking independence from her father. After seven harrowing years in Baltimore, filled with a roller coaster ride's worth of ups and downs in her professional career, coupled with the humiliation she experienced in a relationship that was heading nowhere, Oprah had developed the strength to stand completely on her own, win or lose.

WLS-TV was anxious to have Oprah assume chores as host of "A.M. Chicago" immediately. Its rotation of temporary guest hosts was causing a serious ratings erosion for "A.M. Chicago." To WLS-TV's dismay, Oprah was contractually obligated to continue appearing as co-host of "People Are Talking" until at least December, and WJZ-TV's executives made it clear that they had no intention of granting her an early release without first finding a suitable replacement. In the meantime, WLS-TV would have to make do with continued guest hosts for "A.M. Chicago." Unfortunately, this only created an environment that made it possible for "Donahue" to gain even more viewers.

111

Oprah's last days at WJZ-TV were sentimental and teary-eyed, not only for Oprah, but also for the coworkers who had come to know Oprah and had developed a special fondness for her. She has said more than once that she grew up at WJZ-TV. As her final days drew toward a close, this became increasingly more apparent to Oprah.

It's safe to say that, on Oprah's last day as co-host of "People Are Talking," a lot of Kleenex was used in Baltimore. A WJZ-TV employee surprised Oprah by writing a special farewell song for her, which she sang on the program. A compilation of clips featuring some of Oprah's finest as well as most touching and humorous moments was also shown. Watching the clips, which flashed before her eyes in rapid succession, Oprah and "People Are Talking's" viewers were able to witness firsthand the growth Oprah had experienced as she changed from an insecure anchorwoman to a successful and confident TV talk-show host. Studio audience members expressed their feelings about her departure. They informed Oprah that not only were they losing a first-rate TV talk-show host, but also they were saying farewell to a friend.

In contrast, Oprah's arrival in Chicago was anything but warm. Like most of the Midwest, Chicago was suffering through a record-breaking cold spell. "This cold was awesome, it was serious cold," Oprah told Luther Young of *The Baltimore Sun*. "I thought I was delirious in the streets! Negroes weren't built for this kind of weather! We start praying for the motherland!"

On a show discussing holiday blues in 1986, Oprah took a call from a woman who said she was new to Chicago and worried about being alone on Christmas. Oprah, recalling her arrival in Chicago three years earlier, said, "When I came here I was in the exact same condition. So I went to work in a soup kitchen the first day, like three days before Christmas. And that's what I did for Christmas. It was eighty-two degrees below zero, you see." An image of her first week in Chicago flashed in Oprah's mind and she added, "I remember walking to the corner and gettin' blown down by the wind, and I said, 'Well, this is a sign I'm supposed to go back to the hotel!' "

Another viewer said she dreaded New Year's Eve. "New Year's Eve?" responded Oprah. "You know what? I used to call up the operators and ask them how they were doin'. I called the fire departments, the operator, all the people I knew were on and say, 'Hey, how ya doin'? Happy New Year!' "

Oprah's first New Year's Eve in Chicago, however, wasn't spent holed away in her hotel room. WLS-TV executives had decided to have Oprah make her Chicago debut at the traditional State Street New Year's Eve celebration, which the station had covered live for years. It was a big change from the "What's an Oprah?" campaign WJZ-TV had mounted to publicize Oprah's arrival in Baltimore and one she appreciated. She told Luther Young, "It was calculated on their part. It's best if you get to know the city first, if people get to like you on your own merits, by word of mouth."

Chicago viewers judged Oprah by her own merits, and in no time at all, tongues all over the city were wagging as people asked, "Did you see the new host on 'A.M. Chicago'? I think her name's Of-ra Winfrey."

10

Oprah's Successful Solo Flight

"There aren't a lot of black people in the Chicago media, and I'm the only one doing what I'm doing. When I came on the air here, it was like you could hear TVs clicking on all over the city."

"**I** had my own little game plan for Chicago," Oprah told P. J. Bednarski of *The Chicago Sun-Times*. "In one year, I'd walk down the street and people would know who I am. In two years people would watch me because they'd like me. In three years, I'd gain acceptance—you know, I'd see Phil Donahue getting a pizza and I'd say, 'Oh, hi, Mr. Donahue. I watch your show sometimes.' "

One month after Oprah's debut as "A.M. Chicago's" new host, the program logged its strongest ratings in years, attracting a 7.0 rating and a 25 share of the audience. Exactly one year before, "A.M. Chicago" was averaging a 5.0 rating and a 19 share. Not only was "Donahue" outrating the former "A.M. Chicago"; reruns of an old situation comedy on NBC's WMAQ-TV were also drawing better ratings. With Oprah at the helm, "A.M. Chicago" changed its format dramatically and the audience responded with enthusiasm.

Four months after Oprah's arrival *Variety* reported, " 'A.M. Chicago,' with new host Oprah Winfrey, has increased its rating and share by more than 50 percent from a year ago and in the process has put a severe ratings dent in the New York-bound 'Donahue' show on WBBM-TV and 'The Facts of Life' on WMAQ-TV."

"I'm not surprised it happened," WLS-TV's general manager Dennis Swanson told P. J. Bednarski. "The surprise is how quick it happened. She's natural on television."

"When Oprah got her own show," says Debbie DiMaio, "it was like bringing a child to an open schoolroom—you know, the open classroom, where you get to go crazy? Do whatever you want to do? For Oprah it was, 'Here's your chance to do it. Ask any question you've ever wanted to ask. When you want to ask it.' "

Reviewing Oprah's performance as host of "A.M. Chicago," Luther Young commented that she seemed more relaxed than in her Baltimore days. "I am more relaxed because I have been allowed to be myself here more so than before," explained Oprah.

It took a few weeks before "A.M. Chicago's" production staff fully appreciated that Oprah functioned best when she was allowed to be herself, completely unrestricted. During one of Oprah's earlier shows as the new host of "A.M. Chicago," Tom Selleck appeared as a guest. For a local TV talk show, having the star of a top-rated prime-time TV series was considered quite a coup and the staff wanted to see that everything ran like clockwork for the huge audience "A.M. Chicago" was sure to attract. Carefully prepared questions such as "What are your faults?" and "What's in your refrigerator?" were written for Oprah to ask. Introductions were also scripted and displayed prominently on cue cards, telling Oprah exactly what she should say at the beginning and closing of each segment. Meeting Tom Selleck, Oprah impulsively asked, as her very first question, "Did you know your eyes are the color of a crystal blue sea?" The audience loved it and Oprah, given the circumstances of the strict format set before her, tried to perform as best she could.

At the staff meeting immediately following the show, Oprah expressed her dissatisfaction over the instructions she was expected to follow. She explained that she didn't like to work from a script because it confused her. "It just doesn't work for me. It throws me totally off balance. How can I ask a question if I already know the answer? I look like I'm faking it."

Following the Tom Selleck interview, "A.M. Chicago's" staff did away with the prepared questions. Instead, Oprah was given a packet of material at the end of each day with information pertaining to the following morning's show. Oprah could read it, familiarize herself with the subject, and decide on her own what to ask.

"One of Oprah's great gifts," says Debbie DiMaio, "is her ability to ask the question that is on the tip of the tongue of everyone watching at home. She's your next-door neighbor. And when you're sitting down watching TV with your next-door neighbor she'll turn to you and say, 'Hey, what do you think about that?' " Debbie added, "I hear this all the time from audiences, they come to me and say, 'You know, I feel like I know Oprah Winfrey. I feel like she's a friend of mine. And she always asks what I want to know.' She goes into the show watching it as it's revealed to her, as it is to the studio audience and the viewers at home. In other words, she's not caught in some strict format. If it occurs to Oprah that she wants to ask a question about someone's childhood, then she asks. Everything is very instinctive with her. Usually, she's right on the money."

Discussing the ideal situation for conducting an interview, Oprah told Jon Anderson of *The Chicago Tribune*, "I'm best when I can sit down, have a conversation, and develop some sort of insight."

Oprah's arrival at WLS-TV was only one of three major programming changes general manager Dennis Swanson had instituted in the early winter of 1984. He persuaded Floyd Kalber, a popular Chicago anchorman for more than ten years, to head WLS-TV's revamped six o'clock news report. Kalber had left Chicago in the late seventies to anchor the news reports on NBC-TV's "Today Show." During the mid-seventies, he was teamed to co-anchor WMAQ-TV's weeknight newscasts with a then twenty-four-year-old newcomer from Indiana, Jane Pauley. WLS-TV had also acquired the Chicago rights to the syndicated version of "Wheel of Fortune" and scheduled it immediately following its six o'clock news. Within weeks, WLS-TV's six o'clock newscast was the top-rated news show in its slot and "Wheel of Fortune" outrated not only its competition, but also many prime-time network TV shows, and often landed in the top ten.

A fourth change at WLS-TV, one that involved Oprah, never took off. Since the late seventies, WLS-TV, with its strong lineup of afternoon soaps, has dominated the Chicago market, often attracting a larger share of the audience than WBBM-TV and WMAQ-TV combined. Wanting to capitalize on this large audience, Dennis Swanson decided to slot a syndicated series, "Woman to Woman," after "General Hospital" and follow it with an expanded four o'clock newscast. Negotiations were under way to lure a popular anchorwoman away from WMAQ-TV, but, in the meantime, the station was without a news personality to co-anchor its four o'clock news. Realizing that Oprah had news experience, Dennis Swanson tapped her to co-anchor the program's trial run, a move Oprah wasn't thrilled with.

"I didn't want to do the news," she says, "and had made

it clear that I didn't want to do it." However, as a favor to Dennis Swanson, Oprah consented. It was the last time she has ever anchored the news.

"That was part of the growth to get to where I am now," Oprah explains. "I am a better interviewer and talk-show host because of it. All of those fires, chasing ambulances, plane crashes, political hearings, and gas and electric company meetings—all that stuff—helped to get me where I am. It also helped me to shut people up when I need to. That's part of the art, too. It's give-and-take because people come on and they want to tell you what they want to tell you. And you want them on so they can tell you what *you* want them to tell you. So you have to be able to say, 'Okay, we've heard enough about that now,' without actually saying it."

Oprah has said that she deliberately chose not to view past tapes of "A.M. Chicago" with Robb Weller as host when she came to Chicago. She didn't see the point. From what she understood, she and her predecessor had completely different styles.

Oprah did reveal, however, that there was a period when she found herself watching Phil Donahue. "I used to watch him all the time," she said. "I'd tape 'Donahue.'" Oprah said she finally had to stop doing it, though, because, being a great imitator, she worried that she might start confusing his style with hers. "There was a point when I noticed I was doing the same thing with the microphone that he does and I said, 'Phil does that.' One day, on the air, I said, 'Hey, would you help me out here?' And then I said, 'Oh boy! I've been watching too much of Phil.'" Oprah adds, "I have the greatest respect for him, though. I learned how to do what I do because of him."

It was Oprah's own style of interviewing that caused some national celebrities to be nervous about appearing on "A.M. Chicago" with her. Christie Brinkley revealed to the show's staff that she had heard Oprah could be brutal. "Brutal?" asked a surprised Oprah. The more appropriate term should have been "brutally blunt."

When Dudley Moore appeared on the show Oprah asked him about the technical difficulties of making love to taller women. "Fortunately," responded a good-natured Moore, "the extra length seems to be in their legs." Later, Oprah commented, "I'd marry Dudley Moore tomorrow! I don't know a whole lot of guys shorter than me, but I'd marry that Dudley Moore tomorrow. He's wonderful. He's so funny, just naturally funny. And sincere."

Interviewing Sally Field, Oprah asked if her former lover, Burt Reynolds, wore his toupee to bed. Oprah realized she had gone too far when she saw a shocked look come across Sally's face. During a commercial break Oprah approached her and apologized for having asked the question.

"What comes naturally is what works, so I just keep doing it," Oprah told P. J. Bednarski of *The Chicago Sun-Times*. "Most talk-show people ask talk-show kinds of questions. They're formal. They sit with their legs crossed. They *behave* themselves."

One of the fringe benefits of hosting a TV talk show is you get to meet interesting people you've always admired. When Candice Bergen was scheduled to appear on "A.M. Chicago" to discuss her book, *Knock Wood*, Oprah looked forward to meeting her. "I had read *Knock Wood* and I wanted to sit down and have a nice talk with Candice. I realize this is probably difficult to do on television and be insightful, because that doesn't play in the suburbs at nine in the morning."

Unfortunately, the morning Candice Bergen appeared on the show, Oprah was suffering from a bad case of the flu. Consequently, she felt it adversely affected the interview. "I was not good with Candice Bergen," says Oprah. "She was excellent. She is the definition of a class act if ever there was one." Recalling the live interview, Oprah says, "There were moments when my vision, it was like I was seeing double. My head hurt. My energy was off. I was not in sync. I was really, really off."

One of the most memorable celebrity interviews Oprah

recalls from her early days of "A.M. Chicago" was when former Beatle Paul McCartney was a guest. "I was the biggest Beatles fan," says Oprah, as she recalls growing up in Milwaukee. "I had all their posters up on the wall, just like everyone else did. So, I'll tell you the truth, when I heard I was going to interview Paul McCartney—I mean, for a week I was so worried about what I'd ask him. And I never think about what I'm going to ask—ever! The red light comes on and I say, 'Well, something has to happen here.' But with Paul McCartney it was like, 'What am I gonna say? What should the first question be?' " Finally, on the morning of the interview, Oprah decided the best course of action would be to just do "what comes naturally." She told Paul McCartney, "Paul, when I was a kid growing up I had all the Beatle posters on my wall. Every morning I'd go to the posters and I'd say, 'Dear God, please let me meet Paul one day.' " Paul McCartney smiled, listening appreciatively as Oprah told her story, and then she said, "I wanted to know, all that time were you thinking about me too?" Recalling the interview with fondness, Oprah said, "That's how the interview started and we had a hoot of a time, just a hoot of a time."

When asked to recall which celebrity interviews made her most nervous during her first year as host of "A.M. Chicago," Oprah answered that there were two, and then added, surprisingly, that Paul McCartney wasn't one of them. "Paul McCartney didn't even count because I thought to myself, 'Oh my God! I finally met him! Now I can die in peace.' "

Instead, the two interviews that made Oprah's heart skip a beat, and her breathing shallow, were ones she did with the two women she considers her mentors. The first was Maya Angelou, author of *I Know Why the Caged Bird Sings*. Oprah says, "I was terrible with Maya Angelou. I stumbled through the whole thing."

The second interview was with the woman Oprah once

maintained she most wanted to be like when she grew up, Barbara Walters. "I thank God for Barbara Walters," Oprah says. Speaking for female television journalists she adds, "I think that without her none of us would be here. She's a pioneer and she paved the way for the rest of us."

Recalling that first interview with Barbara Walters on "A.M. Chicago," Oprah says, "It was terrible, because I'm not really good with people that I like—not only like, but am enamored with!" Oprah doesn't even remember the first question she asked Barbara Walters. Instead, all that was going through her mind was, "Finally, I get to meet Barbara Walters!"

Oprah says she lost the one thing during the interview that's important for any journalist to maintain—her objectivity. "I kept saying, 'Barbara, you're so pretty!' I mean, that's real objective." Oprah jokingly recounts that she also made such comments as 'I love your pink sweater! Where'd you get your shoes?' " At the time, Oprah didn't regret her actions because she firmly believed that, one day, she would get another shot at interviewing Barbara Walters.

Although Oprah has had some memorable celebrity interviews, Debbie DiMaio says, "We like to stay away from celebrity-oriented shows. Oprah does better with controversial shows, with guests that have some kind of passion, and emotion, and a story to tell, something that has happened to a person and they've made it through. We call them true-life stories. Usually, they're very emotional stories. We always kid her, but Oprah has had such an incredible life that, no matter what topic we do, it's usually something that has happened to her, in some way or another. If we're doing a show on anything from child abuse to growing up in a broken home, all of that stuff has happened to her. So, unlike the usual blond bubble-headed TV talk-show type who can just turn to the person and say, 'Oh, how sad. I feel so sorry for you,' here's a talk-show host who can say, 'I was there. I can relate to this. Let me tell you how I feel also.' I think that's what makes her special."

Oprah was once asked if there was anything from her past that was difficult to discuss. She answered, "No, there is nothing. I don't have any trouble discussing anything from my past, including being sexually abused as a child and growing up feeling unloved and looking for love in all the wrong places and just being a frustrated teenager. I think that we basically all are the same. I had a difficult childhood, and other people have difficult adulthoods. I think we are all victimized or feel victimized at some point in our lives, but we have to be responsible for claiming our own victories. So there is nothing that I feel embarrassed or ashamed about, past or present, because I try to live my life so that other people can see the light in me. And that's all anybody can do—be the best they can be."

"I think Oprah's a gifted person," says Debbie, "and with that comes a lot of intuitiveness, a lot of special kind of sensitivity. I think she also has a little bit of 'psychicness' in her, in the fact that she has a lot of feel for people. She's a real quick judge of people and a real accurate judge of people. Say, for instance, that someone would walk into the room. She can give a really quick analysis of what that person's about, whether she knows them or not."

Besides entertaining her audience, Oprah has also attempted to use her position as a talk-show host to help others. She recalls an early "A.M. Chicago" show she did discussing agoraphobics, people who fear leaving their houses. "We had given out a number and this woman called the number, but no one there was able to help her because she lived too far away and they were going to charge her all this money." The woman called Oprah back and said she didn't know what to do next. "I talked to that woman for two weeks straight," says Oprah, "until I found someone to help her. Finally, a minister friend of mine talked her out of the house. She had been in the house for two years."

On another show, discussing self-abusers, people who habitually cut or physically hurt themselves, Oprah received a call from a woman who became emotionally unraveled on the air. She identified herself as a self-abuser and then said that her husband was out of work, one of her children had cancer, and that she was so frustrated she didn't know where to turn for help. "It was a very emotional call," says Debbie, who recalled that not only the entire audience but everyone in the control booth was in tears as they listened to the woman.

Oprah told the woman that she was concerned about her, and that she truly wanted to help her, but was worried that by continuing their conversation live on the air the show could veer into a form of television therapy. Instead, Oprah instructed the woman to give her home phone number to an associate producer and promised that she'd call her back as soon as the show was over. Oprah realized this was a risky step to take. If she got too involved, what if the woman became dependent on her for help? What if many others called in and expected that kind of personal therapy or other forms of direct support from Oprah? Oprah says that, in fact, that had often happened to her in Baltimore. "People would call and they'd need shoes for their children, or clothes." For a while, Oprah even attempted to accommodate their requests, but finally realized that "there are just so many checks you can write." With this woman, however, Oprah sensed the situation was more extreme. "There are times when you know you can make a difference."

Oprah stuck by her word to call the woman and they talked for more than two hours. During their conversation, Oprah learned that, not only was the woman's husband out of work and that their oldest son had cancer, but also that another child was suffering from an undiagnosed disease and they were about to lose their house. "I was thinking about writing her a check," admits Oprah. "But how much is enough when you have every problem in the world?"

Instead, Oprah told the woman, "Look, I wish there was something I could do for you. I'd like to take you to lunch, or to dinner, and we can talk about this." The woman declined Oprah's invitation, but said she felt better just being able to talk to someone.

"Ya know, I think, gee, it's a small thing for me to do," says Oprah. "But when I hear from people like this—and I think probably that is one of the assets of the show—I feel like everybody else."

Oprah says that people would come up and ask about the woman for weeks after the show on self-abusers aired. Calling the woman back, Oprah said, "Look, how are things going? People have been calling in. They're really concerned. How are you?" She talked to her for forty-five minutes.

During their second conversation the woman told her, "Oprah, what I didn't tell you is that when I made that phone call to your show, I had pills in one hand and alcohol in the other. I was going to take them. But because of your show I didn't. I haven't had the courage to throw them out yet. They're still in the cabinet. But I didn't take them, and I'm taking things one day at a time."

"Now is that the beauty of television?" asks Oprah. "I said to myself, if I do nothing else in my life, that was a big positive. I mean, that's why we're born. I'll never forget her."

Oprah's early "A.M. Chicago" shows also took some unusual turns. On one show, Oprah got a chance to sing, and rehearsed for a full day with a choreographer on a dance number to accompany the song. On a show exploring blindness, Oprah spent twenty-four hours pretending to be blind. "A.M. Chicago" cameras followed Oprah

124

through her day as she attempted to eat, take walks, and do other seemingly simple tasks that sighted people take for granted. On a Michael Jackson look-alike show, Oprah joined in the fun by wearing a bright red dress and dark sunglasses. On another show, Oprah interviewed a woman who claimed she had been seduced by seven priests. "I asked her, 'What did you do when the priest pulled his pants down?' That's the first thing that came into my mind . . . and I thought, 'Maybe I shouldn't have said those things.' "

On a show asking, "Does Sexual Size Matter?" Oprah told the audience, "If you had your choice, you'd like to have a big one if you could. Bring a big one home to Momma!"

When the Ku Klux Klan appeared on the show Oprah asked if they'd be interested in having lunch after the show. They declined her invitation. "I only wanted to eat," says Oprah. "Some people said, 'I would have slapped them.' But what you have to understand is that when the show is over, those people are still gonna be the Klan and I'm still gonna be Oprah. You can only hope to expose racism for what it is."

Probably the show that made Oprah most uncomfortable was when nudists appeared on "A.M. Chicago." "We had these nudists on—I mean actual naked people," Oprah told *Cosmopolitan* magazine. "I pride myself on being real honest, but on this show I was really faking it. I had to act like it was a perfectly normal thing to be interviewing a bunch of naked people and not look." Although the guests were in full view of the studio audience, the home viewing audience saw only shots of them above their shoulders. "I wanted to look into the camera and say 'My God! There are penises here!' But I couldn't. And that made me real nervous."

"What was your most frightening show?" Oprah was once asked.

"It was a show we did on satanic cults," answered

Oprah. "There was a call from a fifteen-year-old boy who had been part of a cult for ten years. He said he had witnessed human sacrifices and knew that one day he would have to sacrifice himself. He was going to a local high school and was still an active member of this cult. What is frightening about that is to realize that it is not just an idea you have in your head, but that satanism is prevalent, and we, as a society, are so unaware of it."

As Oprah reached her first half-year mark in Chicago, P. J. Bednarsky interviewed her about her success in *The Chicago Sun-Times.* "I'm gonna be okay," she said. " 'Cause I've been here six months and I'm still feeling great. It's the happiest time of my life, and you know, usually you don't feel good for six straight months. I'm just wondering, when is something horrible going to happen?"

Seven months into Oprah's run as the new host of "A.M. Chicago," WLS-TV, impressed by the show's strong ratings, expanded it from thirty minutes to a full hour. It was on one of Oprah's first one-hour shows that she received her first major criticism from the Chicago press. Porno film stars had been invited to appear on "A.M. Chicago" to discuss their work. At one point, one of the guests called the graphic lovemaking that takes place in the films the "money shot." Later, after listening to one of the guests describe the long hours they worked, Oprah asked, "Don't you ever get sore?"

Shortly after the show aired, Bednarsky wrote a column criticizing both Oprah and "A.M. Chicago." His comments included, "The Ask-the-Porn-Stars program, amazingly, carried not a minute of discussion in which Winfrey stated, asked, or even worried that these X-rated stars were, in fact, cheap hucksters, talentless, sleazy skin-traders. She barely wondered if these films demeaned women."

Later, he added that when one of the guests "uttered an unprintable slang expression for male ejaculation, it was an indication that Winfrey had lost the ability to guide the conversation—which Donahue can do—in favor of the cheap thrill.

"For someone with the natural talent of Winfrey, it was telling evidence she's got some growing up to do."

Bednarsky concluded his column with, "The porn stars, every so often, expressed sadness that no one takes their work seriously. And those were words Winfrey should have listened to. She's completed seven months of hosting 'A.M. Chicago' largely devoid of the wooden-stick mentality of her predecessors. But what she'll always be known for is the 'money shot.' That's a shame."

When asked how she responded to criticism Oprah once answered, "It depends. If I feel the criticism is justified, I respond well, and I use the criticism to grow from, and I let it work for me. If I feel that people are just talking out of the sides of their heads, and it's unjustified, or that a person has made a prejudiced judgment or an incorrect perception about my character, then I get upset."

Discussing the criticism she received, not only on the porn show, but also on "Does Sexual Size Matter?" Oprah says, "In terms of being very careful about what I say, I have decided to not be as much 'Oprah' as I can be when it comes to those kinds of shows, to think before I say things, because normally I don't. That's where 'Don't you get sore?' came from. I was just thinking, Oh my God! This woman said 'sometimes we work thirteen hours a day!' Well, how in the world do you do it?" Oprah also added that if a situation came up again where she was as dumbfounded as the audience, she would just tell them and then cut to a commercial.

"I think she's extremely entertaining, facile," Bednarsky told Luther Young of *The Baltimore Sun*. "She has a way of being so natural on the air. Occasionally, that gets beyond her. It's pure honesty, I think. She just has to watch what she's doing."

"Oprah's at her best when she's being sensitive and not

sensational," said *The Baltimore Sun*'s TV critic, Bill Carter.

By the end of Oprah's first year as host of "A.M. Chicago," Phil Donahue, after more than ten years in Chicago, moved his show to New York. Although some Chicago columnists suggested that Oprah was responsible for the change, she says, "Marlo, not me, made him move." At a farewell banquet Phil Donahue wished Oprah luck, but added, "just not in my time slot!"

Almost a year to the day Oprah made her debut as the new host of "A.M. Chicago," *Newsweek* magazine did a full-page story on her success. It was the first national story on Oprah and one that she said "opened a lot of doors for me."

11

First "Tonight Show" Appearance

"Nothing is supposed to happen on 'The Tonight Show' that you don't know is supposed to happen. They give you a script. They tell you what you're going to be asked, so you know ahead of time. You go over the script before you go on."

Oprah was thrilled with the exposure she received from the *Newsweek* piece, and said she loved the writer, Pat King, for doing it. Oprah found herself uncomfortable, however, when the magazine described her as "nearly two hundred pounds of Mississippi-bred black womanhood, brassy, earthy, street smart and soulful."

"I did not like it," says Oprah. "I don't like the term 'street smart.' I think it's a term that gets put off on black people a lot. Rather than say intelligent, it's easier to say we're street smart and that kind of explains a lot of things. 'Oh, well, she made it because she's street smart.' Well, I am the least of the street smarts. I've never lived on the streets. I don't know anything about it. I never was a hustling kid. I mean, I had my days of delinquency. But I was never like a hustling kid, or streetwise. I wouldn't last ten minutes on the streets."

The *Newsweek* article caught the attention of some very influential people, including the staff of NBC-TV's "The Tonight Show." Soon after the article appeared, Oprah received a call asking her to make an appearance on the show. "After the call came, I went home and sat in my window and cried," Oprah told Luther Young of *The Baltimore Sun.* "I really don't know what I did to deserve this."

Oprah was booked to make an appearance with guest host Joan Rivers at the end of the month. She was also promised that she could make a second appearance with Johnny Carson. For two weeks prior to her first appearance, Oprah said she was so nervous she couldn't even watch "The Tonight Show."

The *Newsweek* article, combined with the "Tonight Show" appearance, prompted P. J. Bednarsky to ask Oprah in *The Chicago Sun-Times* if she might be getting "too big for her britches."

"I can tell you I'm more than a little offended by the question," Oprah responded. "Anyone who knows me knows that can't happen to me. I'm offended by the whole 'la-di-da, chichi, poo-poo' syndrome. I mean, it offends me. I think the reason people say that is they know if they got this much attention, they'd be crazy."

Oprah recalls an incident when she did worry that other people, particularly her coworkers, may have thought that she was becoming affected by the attention. She says the incident took place shortly after the *Newsweek* article appeared and she had been booked on "The Tonight Show." "We did a show and I didn't approve of the guest," Oprah explains. "I didn't think he should have been there. I was fighting for my life for an hour.

"After the show, at our meeting, I just seethed. We had words, me and the producer. And then I worried, because I knew what everybody was thinking: 'There it is. She's got a big head.'"

Oprah's first "Tonight Show" appearance was scheduled for January 29, which, coincidentally, was the same day she'd be celebrating her birthday. Since Oprah was taping a special "A.M. Chicago" show that same week, to promote ABC-TV's upcoming mini-series, "Hollywood Wives," she and an "A.M. Chicago" crew flew to Los Angeles two days before her scheduled "Tonight Show" appearance. Taping the "A.M. Chicago" shows kept Oprah busy most of those two days and gave her little time to think about her upcoming shot at national television exposure.

"A.M. Chicago" taped a show featuring Oprah sharing a limousine ride with Jackie Collins, author of *Hollywood Wives*, who pointed out the popular haunts of Hollywood's rich and famous celebrities. One couldn't help but wonder what thoughts ran through Oprah's mind that morning. Was she impressed by the fact that she was cruising down Rodeo Drive, in a chauffeur-driven limousine, with one of America's most successful writers? Or did she think about what she and Joan Rivers would talk about on "The Tonight Show" that evening? Her mind may even have wandered back to the first time she visited Hollywood, when she was a fourteen-year-old girl running her hand along the stars on Hollywood Boulevard and dreaming about one day being famous.

"I understand that nothing happens to you without your deserving it or creating it in some way for yourself," Oprah has said. "I believe from the time you are born you are empowered with the ability to take responsibility for your life. And to understand that, I'm telling you, makes me joyous. You can allow yourself to be a victim, or you can be the kind of person who understands that you have to take charge. It gives me great joy to know that I have this much control over my life. It's like soaring over the mountains."

The night before Oprah made her appearance with Joan Rivers, she took time out to dine with longtime friend Maria Shriver and her then fiancé, Arnold Schwarzenegger. "We sat in a restaurant booth and Arnold played Joan," Oprah told Jon Anderson of *The Chicago Tribune*. "He kept pumping me. 'Why are you successful?' 'Why did you gain weight?' But I decided I was going to be spontaneous and have a good time no matter what."

With less than eight hours before her scheduled appearance, Oprah was still without a suitable pair of shoes to wear on the show. She wanted something to match the rhinestone-studded, blue suede gown she had commissioned a Chicago designer to create especially for her first "Tonight Show" appearance. As luck would have it, Oprah found just what she was looking for in a Rodeo Drive shop, a $750 pair of blue, rhinestone-studded shoes. "I'm not an extravagant person," said Oprah. "I went to L.A. and needed some blue suede shoes and couldn't find them. And I was up and down looking for them, too. It was three o'clock in the afternoon and I needed shoes. So I took the first ones I saw."

As the salesclerk finalized the purchase Oprah told him, "You know what? This is a day that will go down in history, because you can know that when I die I will have these shoes on, sir."

One hour after buying the shoes, a "Tonight Show" limousine arrived at Oprah's hotel to drive her to the NBC-TV Burbank studios where the show is taped. Accompanying Oprah was her agent and hairdresser. Since the fiasco in Baltimore, when her hair fell out, Oprah wasn't taking a chance of having someone new and unknown work on her hair, not on one of the most important nights of her life.

Once Oprah arrived at the studio, she went directly to makeup. Oprah said she held off on getting dressed until just before she was scheduled to go on. Referring to the hand-beaded gown she brought with her, she said, "I didn't want to sweat it out so I padded around backstage in my stocking feet."

Ironically, just as people had told Christie Brinkley that Oprah could be brutal, friends told Oprah the same thing about Joan Rivers. Aware of the "fat" jokes Joan had made about Elizabeth Taylor when she was overweight, Oprah asked if the same thing might happen to her. The "Tonight Show" staff told her, "Oh no! She's not going to talk about that. She's going to talk to you about why you're beating Donahue, and why you're doing so well."

"Nothing is supposed to happen on 'The Tonight Show' that you don't know is supposed to happen," explained Oprah. "They give you a script. They tell you what you're going to be asked, so you know ahead of time. You go over the script before you go on."

When two years later, in 1986, stand-up comic Jerry Seinfield appeared on Oprah's show, he told her they had been on "The Tonight Show" together. Oprah responded, "Oh, yeah!" but later confessed that she didn't remember meeting him that night. "The reason I didn't remember," Oprah told her audience, "is because I was such a nervous wreck! Sitting in the little greenroom I don't watch who's on before me because it makes me even more nervous. It reminds me that I'm on 'The Tonight Show.' "

Minutes before her first appearance on "The Tonight Show," Oprah left the greenroom and headed for the bathroom, where she prayed. "One of those 'Dear Heaven, dear Father' prayers," she informed Jon Anderson. "It was 'Dear God. Please help me to be all that I was made to be.' " Oprah then proceeded to take her place behind the famous "Tonight Show" curtain to await Joan Rivers's introduction.

"I was so nervous," said Oprah. "And I'm never nervous. I mean, I've done lots of things and I've never, ever been nervous. I've spoken before thousands and thousands of people and wasn't nervous. I introduced the Jacksons at the Jacksons concert and wasn't nervous. But gee whiz, gee whiz. You think to yourself, 'My God! This is it! Here's the curtain! This is the curtain!' And I'm standing behind the curtain and a stagehand says to me, 'Don't worry, honey. I've seen the best of them throw up right here.' And I said, 'Don't you worry. I'm not gonna throw up!' "

Seconds later Joan Rivers was saying, "I'm so anxious to meet her. They talk about her as streetwise, brassy, and soulful. Please help me welcome—Miss Oprah Winfrey!"

As the audience applauded, Oprah made her entrance. Suddenly, Oprah said, a look glazed over Joan's face. "I thought, 'Uh-oh, she read too much about this Mississippi-bred, soulful, street-smart Negro woman.' I mean, when you hear that you think I'm gonna come out with a chicken and a watermelon wearing a bandanna around my head."

Joan questioned Oprah about growing up on a Mississippi farm and asked about Oprah's winning the Miss Fire Prevention title, which led Oprah to realize they wouldn't be sticking to the script. "None of the questions that were in the script were asked."

Oprah discussed her admiration for Barbara Walters. And then they started talking about diets. "I knew in the back of my mind that it could come up."

"How did you gain the weight?" Joan asked.

"I ate," answered Oprah.

"You're a pretty girl and single," said Joan. "Lose it."

Oprah and Joan then made a bet. Joan would lose five pounds if Oprah would lose fifteen. After that, the show broke for a commercial. When it resumed, a technical difficulty prevented "The Tonight Show's" Chicago audience, which that night was twice its normal size, from hearing Joan's closing comments to Oprah.

Robert Feder, a *Chicago Sun-Times* TV columnist, asked Oprah what they talked about. "Oh, I wish I could say it was something important, but it really wasn't," answered Oprah. "She just said good night to everybody and turned to me and said, 'Okay, we're gonna do it, right? You're gonna lose fifteen pounds, I'm gonna lose five, and you'll come back in March.' And I said, 'Right, we're gonna do it.' "

After the show, Oprah headed for Spago's, where she met with ten friends to celebrate not only her first "Tonight Show" appearance, but also her thirty-first birthday. She told Robert Feder, "When they brought out this chocolate mousse raspberry cake and Quincy Jones started singing 'Happy Birthday' to me, I thought about that Michelob commercial and I said, 'It just doesn't get any better than this.' "

12

Dieting

"Isn't it the worst? I start out every morning with a poached egg and hope. By the end of the day the hope has faded. . . . I luuuuuuv food. You can tell by the span of my hips."

Oprah returned to Chicago eager to begin her well-publicized diet. She told Robert Feder of *The Chicago Sun-Times,* "I've already spoken with 'The Tonight Show' this morning and they want me to call them every week and let them know how I'm doing. Is this enough pressure, or what?"

The same week that Oprah returned to Chicago, Joan Rivers was scheduled to perform at a nearby theater. As a joke, Oprah said she planned to send her a chocolate mousse cake, along with a note reading, "Joan, keep eating."

Dieting was not something Oprah looked forward to resuming again in her life. In a later appearance with Joan

Rivers on "The Late Show," the two again discussed dieting and Oprah said, "Isn't it the worst? I start out every morning with a poached egg and hope. By the end of the day the hope has faded."

"I luuuuuuv food. You can tell by the span of my hips," Oprah said jokingly to *Chicago Sun-Times* reporter Anne Taubneck in an article titled "TV Woman Who Is Not Afraid to Eat." The piece appeared shortly after Oprah began hosting "A.M. Chicago." In it, she described herself as a "potato woman." "I love them fried. I like to bake them, slice them open, and put butter in there with a little oregano."

Oprah also boasted she knew 110 different ways to cook chicken. "My favorite meal is baked or broiled chicken breasts," she explained. "I marinate them overnight in lemon juice and throw in every spice in the cabinet. Then I broil them with lemon juice and Worcestershire sauce. If you broil them until they're really, really crispy, they taste almost like they're fried."

Because she had to be at the studio by 7:45 A.M., Oprah said breakfast often meant an English muffin with cheese, usually eaten very quickly while riding in a cab en route to the studio. She added that by the time the show was finished at 10 A.M. she would be ravenous. "I have a raging hunger. I guess it's because of all the adrenaline that's pumping after doing the show."

While still living in Baltimore, Oprah had revealed that she had lost thirty pounds in two months on a special diet. "For lunch and dinner I would make soup. I steamed broccoli and blended that with bouillon cubes and water, Tabasco, bay leaf, parsley, and thyme so it would be very herby. It's very smooth and creamy, even though there is no cream in it.

"I am one of those people who has dieted and gained, and dieted and gained," she told her audience, "and since I started dieting, have gained seventy pounds. I wake up in the morning, I go and look in the mirror sometimes, and one of the reasons why I realized I don't have a handgun is because I would have shot off my thighs years ago."

"It is an obsession," she told Charles Whitaker of *Ebony*. "It's all any overweight woman talks about. It just happens that I'm in the public eye so people think I talk about it more."

"It's a comfort," she told her audience. "I mean, some people go skiing and they go off to the Bahamas, and that's what they do for a vacation. I'm comforted by pasta."

Oprah also confided to her audience that one of the extremes her perpetual dieting has reached is, "I get on a scale, and depending on whether it's up or down, it's going to be a good day or a not-so-good day, based upon the numbers, the numbers that control your life.

"It's painful. What people don't understand is it really is painful. So when people say to you, 'Why don't you just close your mouth? All it is is willpower. I lost five pounds in three days,' you want to slap them."

Discussing her struggle to lose weight with Stephanie Mansfield of *The Washington Post*, Oprah said, "You don't know what it's like unless food controls your life. For everything I put into my mouth, I either feel like, 'Okay, I'm gonna let myself do this,' or I feel guilt about it. There's not one thing that I eat that I don't think about or regret later."

It was during Oprah's first year as host of "A.M. Chicago" that her new viewers discovered the problems she personally experienced trying to lose weight. She once revealed that she got so hungry during one truly unforgettable diet that she ended up combining the only two foods in her apartment and ate them, a package of frozen hot dog buns and a bottle of pancake syrup.

On one level, Oprah understands the logic behind her desire to reach the "ideal" weight. She told her audience, "I often say in speeches that we have a whole country of women, people who are trying to live a Haines pantyhose existence, because we've heard that gentlemen prefer Haines."

She also shared with her audience a rationalization for her apparent inability to lose weight. "I used to think that the reason I have this whole weight thing is because, I think, once I drop the weight—which I'm going to, so ya'll get ready and envy me, just envy me—one of the reasons I think I've held onto it is because, first of all, it gives people something to feel sorry for you about—'cause you have everything else, but you don't have great thighs, you see. So you use that so that they can't envy you because they have something you don't have."

Oprah has referred to eating as the biggest problem in her life. "I've done Diet Workshops, Weight Watchers, Diet Center, the 'Banana, wienie and egg' diet, the Beverly Hills diet—I was a fool looking for papaya and kiwi—I've done all that. I gained six pounds on the Scarsdale diet. I was out looking for lamb chops on Thursday and boiled egg on Tuesday.

"From what I understand it's part of my security system, because I have always said, 'Well, if this doesn't happen it's because I was overweight.' It's a crutch. And I know it. I'm going to eliminate it as a problem in my life and then I'll have to find another problem."

Thin or not, people have made it clear to Oprah they accept her just as she is. P. J. Bednarsky told Luther Young of *The Baltimore Sun*, "I think one of her big charms in Chicago is that she's actually a little overweight, *not* the perfect-looking TV host."

When fashion designer Earl Blackwell, famous for his annual "Ten Worst Dressed" lists, appeared on Oprah's show he told her, "Oprah, I adore you. I adore what you're doing. And if you lose one pound, as far as I'm concerned, you will lose a piece of the magnificence of Oprah, and don't do it. Don't do it."

Shortly after Oprah's televised bet with Joan Rivers to lose weight she said, "I was out on the street and someone asked, 'How's your diet?'

"I said, 'Oh, I'm hungry now.' "

Oprah added that a little old lady overheard the conversation, came up, and demanded, "Don't you lose another pound! Don't you do it! You won't be the same!"

Oprah responded, "I know. I'll be thinner!"

Once, when an audience member confided on the show that she often felt embarrassed going into restaurants because she thought everyone was looking at her, Oprah said, "It happened to me in Cap Ferrat at one time. I thought it was because I was black or something. I walked in, it was the Hotel de Cap, or something, and there are these Germans in there, and I walked in and everybody put their forks down, and they turned and they looked at me. And this was like—forty pounds ago. So I thought that, 'Gee, they're not used to looking at black people in here.' " Then it dawned on her that they might possibly be staring at her because of her weight. "So I thought, 'Well, I am going to let them.' You know what I did, to the whole room? I curtsied to them, and told them I was Princess Sheba from some island."

Perpetual dieting has also led Oprah to a variety of significant discoveries. "I don't believe that most of us who are overweight are overweight because we've been eating healthily, it's because we eat what we like—barbecue ribs, french-fried potatoes, you know?

"What we are all looking for, I think, is some kind of secret," she told her audience. "And, you know, people say, 'Well, if they could put a man on the moon, they should be able to invent something.' I am still looking for the perfect answer. And that's why every diet book that comes out, I am still prey to that, too, because you read, and you think the answer's in this diet, or the answer's in that diet.

"I was much thinner before I started dieting. And now the goal weight that I wish for is what I was when I first started dieting. When I first started dieting, this is the truth—I first started dieting, this is about five or six years ago, and I was wearing a Calvin Klein size-ten jean. I thought that was bad, because I wanted to get into a size eight. I have those jeans, in memoriam, in my closet. They are there, and every year I say maybe I should give them away. But I won't give them away, because to give away the Calvin Klein size-ten jeans means giving up a sense of hope, meaning that it's all over."

When *People* magazine did a cover story on Oprah in early 1987 she told them, "Women, always black women, three hundred to four hundred pounds, waddle up, rolling down the street and say, 'You know, people are always confusin' me for you.' I know when they're coming. I say, 'Here comes another woman who thinks she looks like me.' "

Two weeks later *People* magazine published a letter addressing Oprah's comments from Joan Spencer, who lived in Ardmore, Pennsylvania. She wrote,

> As a large woman myself, I was shocked by the supposedly sensitive Oprah Winfrey's cruel, vicious remarks about fat people. It's truly sad that her self-hatred causes her to put down her "overweight" viewers. She seems to be saying, "See, I'm not really a fat person; I make fun of them, too." If only Oprah would stop complaining and accept herself as she is, she could show the world that a large woman can be attractive and successful. As it is now, she is worse for our self-esteem than any *Vogue* model could ever be.

Reading Oprah's comments out of context, it was easy to understand Ms. Spencer's feelings. But a comment Oprah once made on her show may help explain her motivation for expressing herself. Oprah told her audience, "All of my friends are thinner. And I tell you what, one of the reasons is because when I see other people who are overweight, I understand, spiritually, we all mirror each other, and I see them as people who are heavier than me, and I say, 'Oh God, that could be me, that could be me.' And there is this fear that it might happen to me."

As a show of support, following Oprah's bet with Joan Rivers to lose fifteen pounds, members of her audience chose to diet with her. "A.M. Chicago's" staff developed a menu plan for them to follow and called it Oprah's Diet. The morning the diet was officially launched, "A.M. Chicago's" entire studio audience consisted of overweight women. Each one wore a sweatshirt emblazoned with the slogan DIET WITH OPRAH!

A sample of the diet read as follows:

BREAKFAST
ice water, with lemon
boiled egg
1 slice wheat toast
glass orange juice
ice water, with lemon

LUNCH
ice water, with lemon
½ can tuna in salad with celery, onions, spices,
    and 1 tbsp diet mayo
sliced tomato and lettuce
1 slice wheat bread
Oprah's puréed broccoli soup
½ orange
ice water, with lemon

DINNER
ice water, with lemon
Oprah's broiled chicken breast: no skin, soaked for an
    hour in lemon juice, Mrs. Dash, spices, curry pepper,
    bay leaf. Wrap in foil and bake.
baked potato with hot sauce and vinegar
6 grapes
ice water, with lemon

That her audience was so involved in Oprah's diet, one year after her arrival in Chicago, that there were people dieting with her, was not only a show of support, but also a symbol of acceptance. In Luther Young's *Baltimore Sun* article, P. J. Bednarsky called it "a phenomenal story for somebody to have come into this market, which has a real xenophobia about people not from Chicago, and make it in less than a year."

Tim Bennett, WLS-TV's program director, added, "I'm a native Chicagoan. I've seen a lot of talent over the years, and usually it takes three, five, six years to build what Oprah has. One of the reasons she's springboarded so fast is that she's in an almost unrestrained format, she has a lot of freedom in the kinds of shows she does. People watch Oprah because they never know what's going to happen."

Joe Ahern, who succeeded Dennis Swanson as station manager in 1985, told Judith Neisser of *United* magazine, "Oprah has this honesty with her audience and her guests that comes through. No matter who you talk to—black, white, rich, poor, male, female, fat, thin—they say, 'You know, she's just like me.' "

"I was walking down the street the other day," Oprah told *Savvy* magazine, "and a woman bus driver pulled her bus over, jumped off it, and ran down the street to shake my hand. The bus was full, and this was five o'clock traffic, but the passengers loved it. Everyone was clapping, and I said to myself, 'This is something! I must be a somebody!' "

"People bring me gifts and leave them with my doorman—bread and cakes, pickles and things; stuff like that," she told *Chicago* magazine. "I walk out the door and there's always a bus there, and everybody waves, and then they tell everybody, 'That's where Oprah lives.'

"I get all kinds of mail. You should see the mail. I still answer it. I hired someone to help me, I can't do it all by myself anymore. And now she needs someone to help her. We've gotten a new computer system that keeps files and so forth, so that you don't have to write every letter over every time. I hate those letters that sound like they

143

were written seven years ago and nobody's revised it since then. So I try to be very personal in each letter.

"People send me things, little dolls and dollettes. Someone made an Oprah doll. Yesterday I got some homemade jam—dietetic."

Despite Oprah's happiness about her growing popularity, she must sometimes draw a line for when she'll give autographs. She told *Savvy*, "Last Sunday I was in church and a deacon tapped me on the knee and asked for my autograph. I told him, 'I don't do autographs in church. Jesus is the star here.' "

One of the nicest things for Oprah that came out of her move from Baltimore to Chicago was that she felt she had found a city she could call home. "I love Chicago. I do think it's the best city in the world, and I've seen half of it, but I think it's the best."

"Chicago's a lot like New York," she commented to David Brenner. "It has the energy of New York, but it's not quite as overwhelming. We can still be surprised in Chicago."

Speaking of New York City, Oprah said, "I feel overwhelmed, frustrated, and out of control in New York. I don't know what to do with myself. I go to New York for the weekend and I stay in the hotel and order Chinese food. I don't know where to go, or what to do, because there's too much and it makes me crazy. On several occasions we've been there, myself and the staff, and we end up in bed by nine. We're some party animals, I'll tell you! But I love Chicago."

One of Chicago's most well-known streets, famous for attracting out-of-towners, is Rush Street, just a few short blocks from Oprah's Chicago home. "It's my street," says Oprah. "It's a great place to meet people, especially when you're one of the most well-known people in Chicago. You're never alone."

Despite the success Oprah experienced as host of "A.M.

Chicago," there was still a part of her life, besides overeating, that created problems for her. After more than a year of living in Chicago, she still hadn't met someone to begin a romantic relationship with. "I haven't given up about getting married," she told Luther Young of *The Baltimore Sun*, "but I've stopped worrying about it. I think when you're an intelligent, successful black woman in the eighties, you're going to have a difficult time finding a mate who is supportive. Mr. Right either will or will not happen for me and I'm not going to stand still waiting for him."

"I would love to have a significant other in my life," Oprah told *Essence* magazine. "That would be wonderful. But everything in life is about timing, and obviously, the timing is not right for me now."

One of the reasons the timing wasn't right for Oprah was because there was still some leftover pain from the stormy relationship she had ended in Baltimore. She told *People* magazine, "Someone tells you you're wonderful, you wonder what's wrong with them. Somebody tells me I'm horrible, I'd say, 'This is wonderful. He understands me. I can grow.' I'd have some arrogant egomaniac dog telling me I was too self-centered, and I'd be thinking, 'Thank you so much for telling me. I need to work on that.' "

When Mike Wallace interviewed Oprah on "60 Minutes" he said, "I would think you'd be a pretty tough lady to handle, ambitious, outfront. You really don't have time, honestly, for a guy. You have time for yourself."

"I think I'd really be great with some guy," Oprah responded. "But I'm not going to go around hoping and praying for it. If it happens, it happens. If it doesn't, I'll get a kitten."

Keeping a sense of humor about the situation, Oprah confided to Chris Andersen of *Good Housekeeping*, "The best place to find single men these days is the frozen-food section of the supermarket, around seven P.M."

On a show discussing how to meet men, Oprah said to one of her panelists, "You're in the grocery-store line. He's ahead of you and he's getting ready to leave. What do you say in that short amount of time so that you can establish some sort of contact later on?"

"Okay," said the panelist, "I'd say, 'You're very attractive. I'd like to spend some time with you.' "

"Oh, I can't say that!" a shocked Oprah screamed as her audience laughed.

Not that Oprah wasn't without an ample supply of men pursuing her. There were problems, however. "The 'Oprah Winfrey' factor always came in," she told P. J. Bednarsky of *The Chicago Sun-Times*. "If it didn't go away, he went away."

One Chicago disk jockey was so interested in winning a date with Oprah that he hired a Goodyear blimp to publicly proclaim his attraction to her. He could have saved his money. Oprah made no secret that she wasn't a fan of casual dating. She told *Cosmopolitan*, "I don't need the kind of dating where you're going out with a man just to go out. If it's not going to be a meaningful relationship—and I can tell you in three minutes if it is or not—then I don't waste my time. So I go through periods where I don't see anyone. Like now. It's not intentional, just sort of de facto celibacy."

"My friends are the office people," she told *Woman's Day*. "We work and we go out to dinner and talk about work. Then we go home and we're back here about seven-thirty in the morning.

"This is all I do. I do this and I do it till I drop. I work, and on weekends I go as many places as I can to speak. I get home and I say, 'What am I supposed to do here?' I guess I could go to the movies. I could. I could do that. I don't."

"I told her I'd be dizzy after all this," Tim Bennett, WLS-TV's program director, revealed to Luther Young of *The*

Baltimore Sun. "But she loves it. She hasn't changed a bit since she came here. She has a personality that is very real and down to earth."

"This is what I've found to be a truth," she once said. "The more I am able to be myself, the more honest and open I am, the more open and honest my guests tend to be. I don't hold anything back and therefore they don't. I take issue with people in this business who pretend they are like everybody else. I certainly know what it's like not to be able to pay the mortgage, but I don't pretend now that I can't afford leather boots. I don't like pretending. When we've had fashion shows, I've said that I have spent eight hundred dollars on a dress, and it causes a lot of resentment. And I've said, 'I'm thankful to you all for helping me to become what I am, which is a rich woman.' Other people in this business don't run into my problems because they don't let any of themselves out. You never know what they can or can't afford because they never tell you."

In addition to hosting "A.M. Chicago," Oprah also found herself averaging five or six speaking engagements a week. One of her favorite audiences is still underprivileged teenagers. She has been known to tell them, "I was like a lot of you. I was a hot little momma."

"The biggest thing I tell them is that you cannot do anything without an education. In this country, at this particular time, we happen to be speaking the King's English. At some other time, maybe, we will change to another language. But right now, it's the King's English. If you are not able to do that, you are already ten paces behind."

Two weeks after Oprah's first appearance on "The Tonight Show," she left for Ethiopia to host a documentary WLS-TV was producing. The station had participated in a famine relief fund for Ethiopia and wanted to show viewers where the money was going and how it was being

147

used to help starving Ethiopians. In a feature story on Oprah in *The Chicago Sun-Times*, P. J. Bednarsky wrote, "At the same time Oprah will be in Ethiopia, 'A.M. Chicago' will be sponsoring a weight-loss promotion. The timing seems terrible."

Considering Oprah's well-publicized fondness for food, Bednarsky asked if she felt it was a problem that WLS-TV was sending her "to a country where there is so little."

"I think the devastation in Ethiopia transcends all that," Oprah responded. "I don't care what anybody says about that."

Oprah did add that she was concerned that her weight might create confusion and considered losing some of it before leaving for Ethiopia. She told Bednarsky, "You go there and you look very healthy, and you imagine, you're out in this desert with these people, who look at you and think . . . what?"

Oprah also acknowledged, with sadness, that there were jokes going around the station about her trip to Ethiopia. Pretending to hold a mike she said, " 'Hi, I'm Oprah Winfrey and standing in front of me are five hundred Ethiopian children.' " She then asked, "It's sick, isn't it?"

To prepare for the trip, Oprah viewed videotapes depicting the devastation in Ethiopia and also read Senator Edward Kennedy's personal account of his visit there, published in *People* magazine. She told P. J. Bednarsky, "What I do understand is once you do see it, nothing you've ever seen or read before will compare to it."

Oprah mentioned that her producer was worried that the trip to Ethiopia could have an adverse effect on her personality. "I know that she feels a lot for people," said Debbie DiMaio. "Given those conditions in Ethiopia, I was concerned that, if she can feel for one person, I cannot imagine Oprah with thousands and thousands of starving people that were about to die. I think she's like a sponge, and to have all those emotions pounded into her . . . I was just a little concerned."

"You don't know me well if you think Oprah will come back and she won't be bubbly anymore," was Oprah's public reply to her friend's concern. Oprah added that she thought the trip would be a life-changing experience.

Oprah recalls two incidents after arriving in Ethiopia where she had to force herself to keep from crying. "The first time was when we first arrived in the city, because it's such a cultural shock. I mean, everybody is walking with donkeys and goats in the street, and there are children carrying eighty pounds of wood on their backs to sell." Oprah said that for each pound of wood carried, the children received a penny. To carry eighty pounds of wood meant the children would be paid eighty cents. "They're beautiful children. And some of them grow up humpbacked because they've never learned to walk straight. That is their life and livelihood. Initially, that was very upsetting."

Oprah said the second incident took place when she and the documentary crew went to the top of a hill in Ethiopia to get a wide shot of the city. "An overall view. And there were these children who came running down from the hill carrying wood on their backs. They saw us and knew we were foreigners. 'For-en-gees,' they called us."

The children began begging Oprah and the crew for money, their voices all pleading at once. Unfortunately, no one had money on them because they had left everything back at the hotel. "It just broke my heart," said Oprah. "I knew how myopic these children were, how limited. They don't know that there's another world out there. They don't even know."

Oprah described one of the greatest joys for the children, to be given a simple bottle of Coca-Cola. "We were drinking these Cokes and we gave it to them. If you could've seen the smiles—from a Coca-Cola! It was an amazing thing. To say that you feel blessed is not even worth saying, at this point, because it's an understatement. Of course you're blessed. But the problem then is, what do you do? What I understood on that hill is that, one at a time, we can make a difference. It sounds trite. But for some reason that thought occurred to me, that you really can. You really, really can. And everybody does what little bit they can. You can't take every child out of the hills of Ethiopia, but you can do what you can to make a difference.

"People say, 'Oh gee, we have problems here. Why are you going over there?' But I really do think the problem of starvation and famine far exceeds anything. When you see children who have not bathed in years, who have only rags—and rags is not even the word—and the rags are infested with lice, it's an amazing thing.

"The basic human rights to food and shelter are denied. I mean, children freeze. Most of the people die between four and five in the morning because that's when it's coldest in the desert. You die because there's not a blanket. So you understand a lot about the world and what matters and what doesn't."

Oprah said the point she tried to make to students about the importance of an education became even clearer to her in Ethiopia. "Although the people are being fed over there, they're fed and then they wait for their next feeding. They're fed again and then they wait again for their next feeding. What I understood was, unless you create a society in which people can take care of themselves, and be responsible for themselves, then you, really, basically have no society. So what's the point? The point is to keep people from starving, obviously. But the point also is to set up some kind of educational system so that people can better themselves. And you can only do that through knowledge. You just can't do that sitting on a hill weaving baskets."

Oprah called the steps WLS-TV and its Chicago viewers had taken to help starving Ethiopians a Band-Aid. "But it's a good Band-Aid because, without the rest of the world, without us, a people would've died. It's so clear. You understand that nobody else is doing anything—that the Ethiopian government is not, for whatever reasons, political and otherwise, so we really have made a difference."

Shortly after her visit to Ethiopia, Oprah received news that would once again put her in a national arena.

13

"That's Sofia!"

"Sofia represents a legacy of black women and the bridges that I've crossed over to get where I am. She's a combination to me of Sojourner Truth and Harriet Tubman and Fannie Lou Hamer, and grandmothers and aunts of mine and other black women who have gone unnamed but who represent a significant part of our history."

"*W*ho reads what when days are hot?" asked *Baltimore Sun* reporter Alice Steinbach in the summer of 1982.

Oprah answered, "This summer I've just finished reading Alice Walker's *The Color Purple*. I read a review of it in *Newsweek* and bought it the same day. It's very different. It's a series of letters written in novel form. I liked it a lot."

Oprah liked the book so much, in fact, that she insisted every one of her friends read it. And if they didn't buy a copy on their own, she purchased extra copies and gave them as gifts. She told Lou Cedrone of *The Baltimore Evening Sun*, "If you got married, you got a copy. If you had a baby, you got a copy. If you divorced, you got a copy. I thought it one of the best books I had ever read."

The Color Purple's central character, Celie, is a victim of sexual abuse, a subject Oprah understood all too well. After first reading the book, she said she thought, "Oh my God! I'm not alone. I was sexually abused as a child and when I read about Celie I couldn't stop. I wrote my own 'dear God' letters (as Celie does) and I identified with all those people. There's magic in that book."

There was also magic involved in the film version of *The Color Purple*, particularly when it came to casting. When Oprah heard a movie was being made of the book, she told Bill Zehme of *Spy* magazine, "What I wanted was to be a part of it. I thought, 'If they would just let me carry water to the set, I'd be ecstatic.' I would have been best girl. Script girl. Xerox person. I would do whatever. It had not occurred to me that maybe I could have a role in it."

The thought, however, had also occurred to other black actors, anxious for work. Before the film rights to *The Color Purple* were even made public, Whoopi Goldberg, who had been performing in a critically acclaimed one-woman show on Broadway, sensed the chances were good a film would be made and knew she wanted to be in on it. She told Nan Robertson of *The New York Times*, "After I read this amazing book, I sat down and wrote to Alice Walker, with a résumé and all my reviews and references, telling her I would go anywhere to audition if this was made into a movie." Willard Pugh, who was cast as Harpo, launched a letter-writing campaign on his behalf to director Steven Spielberg. Actress Margaret Avery said she pleaded with casting director Reuben Cannon to at least let her read for the part of Shug Avery. Although Cannon had been considering Tina Turner for the role, he finally agreed to let Margaret Avery read for it.

In time, Oprah began to think maybe it was possible she could perform in the movie and began waging her own personal campaign to win a coveted role. She prayed nightly to God. One of the reasons Oprah hadn't become a professional actress sooner was because she knew herself well enough to realize she wasn't the type of person who could endure the inevitable rejections actors faced when they made the daily audition rounds. She thought years of having already worked in television had made her ego too big for that.

Something Oprah's New York speech coach once said had also stayed locked away in the back of her mind. The woman had told Oprah she would never make it as an actress because she was only interested in becoming a star. A true actor, she reasoned, was willing to give up everything to become successful. It didn't matter that they had to subsidize their acting aspirations by waiting on tables or answering telephones. That was dedication. It may have been dedication, but it didn't seem very practical or logical to Oprah to give up the generous salary she received as a TV anchorperson just so she could move to New York and wait on tables while hoping to become a successful actress. Oprah knew there had to be a better way. Maybe she wasn't willing to knock on doors, but no one said it wasn't possible she could be discovered. After all, isn't that how it worked for Lana Turner?

As fate would have it, Oprah was discovered in true Hollywood fashion. Quincy Jones, coproducer of *The Color Purple*, had flown to Chicago to testify on behalf of Michael Jackson at a hearing held to determine whether he had written the song "The Girl Is Mine." While in his hotel room, Quincy Jones turned on his television set and caught "A.M. Chicago." Watching Oprah work, Quincy Jones exclaimed, "That's Sofia!" and immediately called Reuben Cannon to arrange an audition with Oprah.

When Oprah received the call from Cannon's people, she

had a funny feeling she would be auditioning for a role in *The Color Purple*, but couldn't be sure because the project was then being called *Moonsong*. The morning she went to meet Reuben Cannon for her initial screen test in Chicago, Oprah was suffering from the flu. During the next few weeks Oprah would film a series of readings from the script, answer questions about herself, and perform improvisations.

But, as ever, Oprah's determination and talent carried her through. Viewing the tapes of Oprah's screen test, director Steven Spielberg was, in his own words, "blown away." Reuben Cannon was directed to call Oprah to set up another audition, this time in Hollywood, where Steven Spielberg would be able to meet personally with her. Cannon tracked Oprah down at a health spa, where she was vigorously attempting to lose weight. He quickly ordered her to stop dieting. In a matter of days, Oprah was on her way to California.

The first time Oprah met Steven Spielberg she said she was so nervous she had to stand with her legs apart to keep her knees from knocking together. The director sensed Oprah's nervousness and immediately did his best to put her at ease. Appearing on "Late Night with David Letterman," Oprah talked about that first encounter. "First of all, you walk into a room and there is Steven Spielberg. It's pretty intimidating, you know. So, the first impression is, 'Oh my God, he's much shorter than I thought he was.' And then once you get over that it's like, 'Oh! He said my name!' And I wanted to remember everything in the room, so that I could at least tell my friends and remember the moment."

Oprah recalled that there was a little popcorn machine in the studio. There was also memorabilia from his films, such as a model spaceship from *Close Encounters of the Third Kind*. It helped that Steven Spielberg didn't dress in an intimidating way; he was wearing a Mickey Mouse shirt and Reebok sneakers.

Oprah tested with actor Willard Pugh, who was cast as her on-screen husband, Harpo. Willard says he was initially nervous testing with Oprah because of her inexperience working in films. "You want your partner to look good because it makes you look good." As part of the audition, Steven Spielberg directed them through a series of improvisations. He wanted to see, for instance, how they would prepare to tell Harpo's father that they were getting married. He also asked them to stage a fight. Then he wanted to see how they related to each other when they made up. "Oprah proved to me that day that she was a pro," says Willard Pugh. "She was really good at those improvisations."

Steven Spielberg agreed that Oprah had a "gift for improvisation." He told the *News American*, "She could pull that character out of nowhere." Steven Spielberg knew Oprah was Sofia, but said he was worried because he now suddenly found himself with a cast of unknowns. Still, he thought Oprah was "dazzling."

"The greatest moment in my life," Oprah told Gary Ballard of *Drama-Logue*, "was when Steven told Willard and me we had the parts. The [Oscar] nomination was not even as great. Maybe the day I was born was greater, but I can't remember that experience."

Willard Pugh recalls that Steven Spielberg had called the two of them together in his office. Just as it had been for the other actors, Willard found the seemingly endless audition process exasperating. He said at one point he became so frustrated not hearing anything that he sent an angry letter off to Spielberg and closed it with a question asking "And what does a white man know about the black experience anyway?" He added that when he told his mother about the letter she said, "Now if he could get people to love a Martian, maybe he could get them to love black folks, too."

When Steven Spielberg told Oprah and Willard they had the parts, the two immediately hugged each other, then jumped around, screamed, and cried. During the frenzy, the spaceship even fell to the floor. Willard said his next impulse was to run down the halls yelling that he had won the part. But Steven Spielberg asked them both to remain quiet with their news because there were still some people who hadn't been told whether or not they'd been cast in the film.

"To be cast in *The Color Purple* and not talk about it?" Oprah said to Gary Ballard. "I was giving some lectures around Chicago at the time to groups of about a thousand people. I'd say, 'I'm not supposed to talk about this but . . . Now don't tell anybody I told you.' I couldn't keep something like that to myself."

Filming was scheduled to begin that summer in North Carolina. Oprah managed to negotiate a release from her contract with WLS-TV to film the movie, but said if she hadn't gotten it, she would have quit "A.M. Chicago"—that's how badly she wanted to be in *The Color Purple*. While Oprah was away, WLS-TV planned to use guest hosts, such as Marilu Henner, and also to run repeats of some of Oprah's most popular shows. The filming was initially scheduled to run six weeks, then it went to nine weeks, and finally to three months.

"I have been an actress in my spirit all my life, and knew that was what I was born to do," Oprah has said. "I feel very blessed that I was discovered by Quincy Jones and that he also had this vision to know that I could do it."

Oprah arrived in North Carolina feeling extremely apprehensive. For starters, she had never before been on a movie set. She joked that she hadn't even taken the Universal tour while in Hollywood. Self-doubts slowly began to gnaw at her. She told *Good Housekeeping*, "For the first time in my life I thought, 'What if I do my best and it's just not good enough?' " It didn't help Oprah's confidence that all of her costars had previous professional acting credits. In fact, Adolph Caesar, who played Mister's father, had even been nominated for an Oscar for his performance in *A Soldier's Story*.

On Oprah's first day on the set, cinematographer Allen Daviau yelled at her because she couldn't find her key light. Oprah said she was absolutely mortified until later Danny Glover, cast as Mister, also missed his light. This comforted Oprah because Danny Glover was an experienced film actor.

Filming *The Color Purple*, Oprah later told her audience, "was the one time in my life I experienced total harmony." On the first day of rehearsals, the cast discovered quite a few incredible coincidences. Margaret Avery shared the same last name as her character, Shug. Whoopi Goldberg and Willard Pugh arrived for the first rehearsal wearing identical sweat clothes. As for Oprah, her named spelled backward was Harpo, the name of her character's husband.

"When I was in the middle of auditioning, screen testing, I said to Steven, Steven Spielberg, if I may drop a name," Oprah told David Letterman, "I said, 'Harpo is Oprah spelled backward. I think that's a sign.' "

"So that was your idea?" David asked Oprah. "You sort of put that in their head and they went back to their office and said, 'Gee, what do you know? She may have something.' "

Although Oprah's career as a TV talk-show host led to her winning a part in *The Color Purple*, other cast members had flexed their acting muscles working in theater, performing in nightclubs, or appearing in supporting roles in TV and film. Prior to filming *The Color Purple*, Danny Glover had completed a role in *Silverado*, which starred Kevin Kline. In addition to her one-woman Broadway show, Whoopi Goldberg had small parts in other Broadway shows, such as *Pippin*, *Hair*, and *Jesus Christ Superstar*. Frustrated at not being able to find work in Hollywood, Margaret Avery had put together a nightclub singing act and had temporarily left the country to tour with it. Weeks before winning a role in *The Color Purple*, she was so close to giving up acting that she had started taking typing lessons, in hopes of finding work as a court reporter.

Whoopi Goldberg was in Los Angeles performing her one-woman show when Steven Spielberg, unable to make a performance, asked her to perform at his studio for him and a "few close friends." Whoopi Goldberg told Jill Kearney of *American Film* magazine, "I thought, 'Hey, I'm going to be in *Raiders of the Lost Ark*.' Well, 'a few close friends' turned out to be eighty people, including Michael Jackson, Quincy Jones, and Alice Walker. And after the show, after I'd had a chance to be blown away by these people, Steven said, 'I'm thinking about doing *The Color Purple*, and it's yours if you want it.'" Trying to remain cool, calm, and collected, Whoopi casually responded, "Oh, oh, yeah, sure."

Ironically, the part Whoopi Goldberg thought Steven Spielberg was offering her was the one she had originally wanted to play, that of Sofia. But Steven Spielberg told her, "No, I see you as Celie."

As with Oprah, Whoopi Goldberg's part in *The Color Purple* seemed naturally to gravitate toward her. Speaking of her own role, Oprah told Stephen Hunter of *The Baltimore Sun*, "I'm convinced that if I had sought *The Color Purple* and called Steven Spielberg and Quincy Jones and said, 'Listen, I really am a wonderful person, give me a chance,' it wouldn't have happened."

Oprah's self-consciousness about her inexperience as a film actress hovered in her mind the first day of filming. "My first day, our first setup, the scene was mine," Oprah told Stephen Hunter. "So I thought, 'I wish I had a day or two to see what they do.' I was quite intimidated."

Although Oprah was judging herself critically that first morning, the other actors had already accepted her as a peer. Because "A.M. Chicago" was a local show, most didn't even know she earned her living as a talk-show host. "No one really knew," says Willard Pugh. "We thought of her as an actress."

"With my show I'm in charge," Oprah told the *News American*. "I'm not accustomed to being intimidated, by big stars or anybody. But this time I was not in control."

Oprah told David Letterman, "It was very intimidating at first."

Curious about Steven Spielberg, David Letterman jokingly asked, "Did you ever have any trouble with the guy?"

Oprah laughed and answered, "No trouble at all."

David Letterman then inquired, "Stuff missing out of your dressing room?"

Once again Oprah laughed and then proceeded to describe her first day of filming. "We were doing the 'Juke Joint' scene. Steven came over to me before the scene and asked if I could cry. You know, Steven Spielberg asks you to cry and you want to give him buckets of tears."

"Now when he says cry," asked David Letterman, "does he mean just the theatrics of crying, or actual tears?"

"He wants a tear falling out of that left eye so when you turn to the camera it's falling right there," answered Oprah. "And I couldn't. I was so afraid that I was not going to be able to cry I started plucking out my lashes and sticking them into my contact lens, and still could not cry." Oprah said she tried to think about all the horrible things that had happened in her life and, still, she couldn't cry.

"When I saw I wasn't going to cry," Oprah told Gary Ballard, "I prayed for death right then and there. Steven said it was okay. We'd do a second take." By the second take, Oprah was still unable to cry. "I thought, 'I'm gonna go down in history as the actress who couldn't cry in a Spielberg movie.' He didn't seem upset but said we'd get it another day. I left the set and cried all afternoon because I couldn't cry for him."

Oprah told David Letterman that Adolph Caesar took her aside later in the day to give her some very practical and useful acting advice. "He said what you have to learn to do is give yourself over to the character, let the character take control. And I never had a difficult time after that."

Wanting to play it safe, Oprah also employed another technique to insure that she'd be able to cry on cue. She told David Letterman, "What I would do when I had to cry is start crying early in the morning, so that I would make sure by the time I had to cry I'd still be crying. I used to cry all day. I did."

"There were tears on the set every day," recalls Willard Pugh. He says even when actors didn't have a scene scheduled for shooting, they'd show up on the set to watch everyone else work. If someone's work was particularly poignant and touching, the actors would applaud and cry.

At the end of each day's shooting, the actors would gather to watch the dailies, footage of the film that had been shot that day. Oprah was totally unprepared for the way she looked in character on film and was not very pleased. She felt her first scenes, which depicted a fight between Sofia and Harpo, were too slapstick and harkened back to the way blacks were depicted in the fifties TV comedy "Amos 'n' Andy." Worried that Oprah's concern with how she came across on screen could end up being a detriment to her performance, Steven Spielberg told her not to attend any more dailies.

Viewing herself in the dailies, however, also had a benefit. "Seeing herself on film for the first time made her more relaxed," says Willard Pugh. It also gave Oprah confidence that she could hold her own with the other, more seasoned, actors.

As filming progressed, Oprah found herself impressed with Steven Spielberg's total involvement in turning himself over to the movie. She said, "He was intensely sensitive to every character. He knew what your character had for breakfast five years ago. He knew how she moved her eyes and how she would be feeling at any given moment, and so how she would react."

Whoopi Goldberg agreed with Oprah's assessment of

Steven Spielberg. In *American Film* she said, "He knew he was the only one who could do it." Whoopi Goldberg then added, "And I think maybe he needed to remind people that he wasn't just a 'techno' director."

"When Sofia makes her first appearance, she is walking three or four feet ahead of her husband-to-be Harpo to meet his father for the first time," said Oprah. "The walk Steven gave me to do was quite powerful, very full of herself. And as I was walking, Steven said, 'Now, I want you to turn around and give Harpo a big smile!' Well, let me tell you, that smile made all the difference between a Trojan woman walking up the road and a woman who's quite sure of herself and kinda kidding around with her man. It made all the difference in the world."

Actually, Oprah felt Sofia was a combination of characters she had been portraying for years. As she told Stephen Hunter of *The Baltimore Sun*, "She represents a legacy of black women and the bridges that I've crossed over to get where I am. She's a combination to me of Sojourner Truth and Harriet Tubman and Fannie Lou Hamer, and grandmothers and aunts of mine and other black women who have gone unnamed but who represent a significant part of our history."

Oprah revealed that when she had first read the book she pictured her Aunt Ida, who had named her, as Sofia and added that she was a great source of strength and inspiration to her.

In an early scene in *The Color Purple*, Harpo confides to Celie that he's having trouble dealing with his headstrong new bride, Sofia. Celie, for reasons of her own, advises Harpo to assert control by beating his wife. Later, an angered Sofia, sporting a blackened eye, confronts Celie. "You told Harpo to beat me!" accuses Sofia. "All my life I had to fight. I had to fight my daddy, I had to fight my uncles, I had to fight my brothers. A child ain't safe in a family of mens. But I ain't never thought I'd have to fight in my own house!"

In a later scene, Sofia is brutally and viciously beaten by the town's white men because she sassed the mayor's wife, who had wanted Sofia to come and work as her maid. After the attack, a bloodied Sofia is arrested and jailed. A few years later she is released, but is forced to work as a maid for the mayor and his wife. Finally, after years of not seeing her children, the mayor's wife accompanies Sofia to the family's farm one snowy Christmas so that she can visit with them. During the filming of the scene, an unscripted yet touching exchange takes place between Sofia and her now ex-husband Harpo.

As a worn-down, white-haired Sofia hobbles up the path to greet her children, she stops and her hand touches Harpo's and their eyes meet briefly. "That moment was improvised," says Willard. He says he and Oprah felt comfortable exploring the moment because Steven Spielberg was always encouraging the cast to find nuances to their characters. Willard Pugh adds that it symbolized the special communication that had developed between him and Oprah. He revealed that, even when they weren't filming scenes together, a special communication and bond existed between them that resembled the relationship a husband would share with his wife.

"Sofia teaches us that there is a great will and power inside us all," says Oprah, "and that you can overcome anything. You can be down, you can even be broken, but there's always a way to mend."

It's a philosophy Oprah tries to share with her audience. On a show featuring people who had been victimized and felt powerless over their situation, Oprah introduced a studio member. She said, "This woman's been sad for a long time. We did a show a year ago and she was sad then." Oprah explained that the woman, who did, indeed, look sad, as well as very frightened, had been knifed in 1985, and then again in 1986. "She has a fear it will happen again in 1987. She expects it to happen. We've gotta get her to learn that nobody has control over your life but you. So, as long as you think it's not you that brings it on, it will come on. What you create for that day, you can create for your life." Oprah could just as easily have been describing the strength and determination Sofia of *The Color Purple* found within herself to overcome her own victimization.

In a scene where Celie finally asserts her independence from Mister, Sofia, after years of silence, quietly begins to laugh. Before you know it, she's telling everyone gathered at the family dinner table exactly how she feels. Originally, Sofia was only supposed to have one line in the scene. Oprah told Thomas Morgan of *The New York Times*, "I remember having sat there for three days of shooting, rocking at the table. Mine was the last angle to be shot. I had been sitting there watching everybody else. I had a lot of time to think about the years Sofia spent in jail, and the thousands of women and men, all the people who marched in Selma, who were thrown in jail and what those years must have been like.

"Sofia finally speaking was a victory for all of us, and for me."

Willard Pugh recalls that the cast was totally surprised, and impressed, by Oprah's improvised speech for Sofia. He says the cameras kept rolling, filming the entire moment. "It was like watching someone preach."

Oprah's college teacher, Dr. Jamie Williams, says when she saw Oprah perform Sofia's major speech in *The Color Purple*, she couldn't help but remember Oprah's dramatic reading from *Jubilee*. She says it had the same intensity behind it, the same emotional pitch that moved Oprah's fellow students when she was a student at Tennessee State University.

Since the cast was filming on location in Monroe, North Carolina, the actors had a chance to get to know each other socially, away from the set. They'd go to movies together at the local theater, share meals in the evening, and frequent the town's one department store. Some nights, they'd rent a banquet room at the hotel where they were staying, set up a portable stereo, and dance the evening away. On other nights, they'd entertain one another with impromptu talent shows. On the film's final day of shooting, everyone, cast and crew included, cried. Oprah told Corinne F. Hammett, "I was really depressed when we finished, because it was the best experience I ever had in my life and I felt never in my life will I be able to top those feelings."

Meanwhile, Oprah had an anxious audience eagerly awaiting her return to Chicago. But first, she wanted to take time out for a little fun.

14

Oscar Night

"It's hard for me to remember drawing water from the well every morning and playing with corncob dolls."

After a summer of filming in North Carolina, Oprah decided it was time to throw herself into a more electrified environment. "I didn't just ease myself back into the fire," she explained to Sugar Rautbord of _Interview_, "I leapt into it." Oprah said she and Whoopi Goldberg headed straight for New York City, where they attended a Bruce Springsteen concert and went on a shopping spree buying an assortment of designer cowboy boots.

The Color Purple was released that winter. Initially, the film had trouble finding an audience because of the stiff competition it received from other Christmas movie releases such as _Beverly Hills Cop_ and _Out of Africa_. It didn't help that the movie received mixed notices from film critics. _Commonweal_ magazine praised the cast for its strong performances, but added, "Throughout the film, there is a painful contradiction between understatement concerning character, and overstatement via photography, especially overly pretty, overly neat, suggestive shots. . . . Some viewers may be able to tolerate Spielberg's methods and continue to care for the characters, despite these manipulations." The review concluded by stating, *The Color Purple* fails to sing; it merely hums the blues."

Gene Shalit, "The Today Show's" film critic, was less negative in his response. He enthusiastically encouraged viewers to see the movie and ended his review with, "It should be against the law not to see *The Color Purple.*"

As with any movie that is based upon a book, there were deviations in the film version from the novel's original story. Some critics took exception to the changes and accused Steven Spielberg of turning Alice Walker's novel into an upbeat Disney film. Ironically, when the movie was being shot, some of the actors expressed their apprehensions to Steven Spielberg about some of the changes that were being made. Ashanti princess Akosua Busia, who played Nellie, told Jack Mathews of *The Los Angeles Times*, "There were moments when I thought, 'Come on, Steven, how cleaned up is this going to be?' "

Akosua then cited the differences between the film's opening and the book's first paragraphs. In the book, a young Celie is being sexually abused by the man she believes is her father. The movie, however, opens on a field of flowers. Akosua thought the film should have been truer to the book on that point, and argued with Steven Spielberg over it. She said he told her, "Look, you can't lose the audience. If we started the way the book starts, people would walk out." After hearing his reasoning, Akosua decided he was right.

Defending the choices Steven Spielberg made, Oprah told Lou Cedrone of *The Baltimore Evening Sun*, "Spielberg said he couldn't include every incident, and that if he had, the film would've been too depressing. As it is, it's a joyous picture, a triumphant one. The essence and spirit of the book are there and that's most important."

The movie was also criticized by some people who felt the black males in the movie were negatively portrayed. A group calling itself the Coalition Against Black Exploitation boycotted the movie and even organized groups to picket outside theaters where it was being shown. Responding to the criticism, Danny Glover told *Jet* magazine, "*The Color Purple* in no way identifies itself as the story of all black men. This is just this woman's story. I have a ninety-one-year-old grandfather and his relationship with my ninety-year-old grandmother has been glorious for seventy years. I have that to draw on. I can't deny that there are Misters. There are homes for battered women, children being molested, and incest happening, not only among black people, but white people."

"Did *The Burning Bed* represent all white women?" asked Willard Pugh.

"If this film is going to raise some issues, I'm tired of hearing about what it's doing to black men," Oprah told Jack Mathews. "Let's talk about the issues of wife abuse, violence against women, sexual abuse of children in the home.

"What the movie did for me, and what the movie is doing for other women who were sexually abused, is pointing up that you're not the only one."

Audiences as well as critics responded enthusiastically to Oprah's performance in *The Color Purple*. Richard Sher, Oprah's former co-host on "People Are Talking," told Stephen Hunter, "If you had to sit down and think of a character for Oprah to really show what she could do, you couldn't write or create a better character than Sofia. Oprah is an extremely talented young woman."

Discussing the audience's reaction to her work, Oprah

told "Entertainment Tonight," "It's that much more enjoyable to me when people say, 'I've gone to that movie and I forgot it was you'—meaning me, Oprah Winfrey. I think, 'God, I did it! I did it!' "

Oprah's performance was rewarded with a nomination for Best Supporting Actress. Her costar, Margaret Avery, was also nominated in the same category. When asked by Gary Ballard of *Drama-Logue* how it felt to be nominated, Oprah responded, "Wondrous, of course, but it's hard to describe. I don't know how I feel about it. It makes it tougher next time out. What do you do to top it?"

The Color Purple received a total of eleven nominations, including one for Whoopi Goldberg as Best Actress. Steven Spielberg's name was not among the nominees for Best Director. It was the first time a movie had garnered as many nominations without including one for the director.

Winning the Academy Award nomination inspired Oprah to set a familiar goal for herself. Appearing in Baltimore one month before the Academy Awards presentation was scheduled to be held, Oprah accepted a local award and told the audience, "I'm dieting now, can't you tell? Thinner thighs by Oscar night, thinner thighs by Oscar night, that's what I keep telling myself."

The success of *The Color Purple* also encouraged Oprah to pursue an acting career in films, as well as to continue hosting her own TV talk show. She credited the movie with giving her a "diversity of paths" to follow. "Having a talk show is a great position to be in because it means that I don't have to do movies to make money and pay bills, and I can choose only the best work. I'm interested in doing roles, creating lives on screen, on film, that in some way help people to better understand themselves and see a bit of glory in other people."

But when asked if she'd ever consider giving up her talk show to pursue a full-time acting career, Oprah answered, "No, I intend to do and have it all. I want to have a movie career, a television career, a talk-show career. So, I will do movies for television and movies for the big screen, and I will have my talk show. I will have a wonderful life. I will continue to be fulfilled doing all of those things, because no one can tell me how to live my life. I believe in my own possibilities, so I can do whatever I feel I'm capable of doing. And I feel I can do it all."

"I am as grounded as anybody you'll ever meet," she told Bill Zehme of *Spy* magazine. "And very, very God-centered. I know who the hell I am! And you have to be responsible for yourself, you see. You get more by doing what comes naturally than you do by efforting to get things! I move with the flow and take life's cues. Let the universe handle the details."

The Academy Award nomination, coupled with Oprah's success as a Chicago talk-show host, caught the media's attention and suddenly she was inundated with requests from the national press for interviews. Although initially happy to oblige their requests, Oprah finally had to put an end to it because, according to her press representative, "she is getting tired of talking about herself."

Referring to Oprah's media exposure, Lou Cedrone of *The Baltimore Evening Sun* asked, "Will all this help Winfrey win that Academy Award? Maybe and maybe not. Winfrey has been highly visible. This same kind of attention has worked against others, and it could work against Winfrey."

Besides the publicity Oprah's success was generating independently, it was reported that Warner Brothers, distributor of *The Color Purple*, was spending huge sums of money promoting the movie in trade papers. "I've never seen anyone spend as much money as *The Color Purple*," one Oscar marketing expert told *Us* magazine. "They've spent like it's a bottomless pit." Warner Brothers' motive for wanting to win top Oscar awards was clear. A major Oscar award could mean as much as ten million extra dollars at the box office.

For an actor, winning an Academy Award usually means more leverage in securing future movie roles at a higher salary. Consequently, it's not unusual for an actor to spend money out of his own pocket to promote himself in the trade papers. Margaret Avery had an ad created for herself that was written in a style that mirrored Alice Walker's prose in *The Color Purple*. The ad read, "I knows dat I been blessed. . . . Now I is up for one of the nominations fo' Best Supporting Actress alongst with some fine, talented ladies that I is proud to be in the company of." One insider speculated that the ad could hurt her chances of winning the Oscar, as well as her film career. Margaret Avery told *Us* magazine, "I took the last money [from her *Color Purple* salary] to remodel my kitchen; it was my new stove," she added, referring to the ad. "If people think it's out of line, as Shug would say, 'F—k 'em.' "

Winning the Academy Award nomination gave Oprah an opportunity to socialize with some of Hollywood's biggest film stars. Recalling that period in her life, Oprah told *Cosmopolitan*, "Getting the Oscar nomination was pretty great. And I guess one of my biggest thrills was walking into the Oscar luncheon and sitting next to Jack Nicholson. He's my absolute favorite actor. I kept saying to myself: 'Self, would you look at this!' "

Oprah also commented in *The Los Angeles Times*, "It's hard for me to remember drawing water from the well every morning and playing with corncob dolls."

Oprah's press agent fielded requests from a number of journalists, including Ron Reagan, Jr., who were asking to spend Oscar day with her. But Oprah wasn't interested. She said, "I turned them down for the same reasons I'm not wearing a purple gown. If you lose, you look totally ridiculous after they followed you around all day with a camera crew. And I'd look pretty stupid sitting there in that purple gown if I lost."

As Oscar day grew nearer, it became apparent to Oprah

she wasn't going to lose the weight she had set for herself shortly after receiving the nomination. She told her TV audience, "I said, 'I'm going to lose weight, I'm going to lose weight.' And then two weeks comes, and you need to lose fifty pounds by Monday. And so you know it's not going to happen, and so what does that do? That sends you off on another binge because you're not going to lose it the next day."

Three days before Oscar night, Oprah told *The Nashville Banner*, "I was wanting to lose all this weight so I could fit into the gown, and suddenly it dawned on me—what you need to do is lose thirty pounds in two days!

"So then I figured I might as well eat and enjoy the weekend." Unfortunately, this created further problems for Oprah.

In a long-distance telephone press conference with Nashville reporters three days before the Oscar ceremony, Oprah was asked what she'd be wearing. "Would you believe it? I don't know and it's Friday already," Oprah responded.

Oprah then added, "I do know it's gold and ivory. And it's shiny, with beads. Tony Chase, who does all of Patti LaBelle's gowns, is designing it. I've bought shoes, a bag, earrings, everything to go with it. But I won't see the gown until Sunday."

That Sunday, Oprah registered at the Beverly Wilshire and called Tony Chase. A short time later he arrived with her gown. "I tried on the gown," Oprah told Lyn Tornabene of *Woman's Day*. She added that the gown fit fine. Wanting to make further adjustments on the gown, such as tapering it at the knee, as well as hemming it, Tony Chase told Oprah he wanted to take the gown with him.

The following day, Tony Chase returned with the gown, having made the necessary adjustments. Five minutes before she was scheduled to leave for the ceremony, Oprah put the gown on and discovered, to her horror, that it didn't fit. She struggled to squeeze herself into the gown, but to no avail. Finally, she said, four people had to lay her on the floor so that they could pull the gown on her. When they stood her up, Tony Chase reportedly asked, "Do you have a girdle?"

Oprah responded that she did not bring a girdle with her, and there wasn't time for anyone to run out and buy one for her.

When the limousine arrived to take Oprah to the ceremony, she swore that they had to lay her down in the back of it. The whole way to the Dorothy Chandler Pavilion, Oprah wondered how she was going to get out. She knew there would be cameramen present, waiting to take her picture. Finally, she asked the driver to stop the limousine a block away from the Dorothy Chandler Pavilion and, she said, she rolled herself out. "Isn't that unbelievable?" Oprah asked Lyn Tornabene. "I sat in the gown all night and I couldn't breathe. I was afraid the seams were gonna bust. If I leaned forward I cut off my windpipe and I could just pass out."

To make matters worse, Oprah said, there were six standing ovations during the ceremony and every time the audience stood up, she literally had to be pulled out of her chair. As for the moment when the nominees would be called for Best Supporting Actress, Oprah had three days earlier said, "I'm not the least bit nervous about it, actually. I don't get nervous about something when I have no control over it. Besides, my category is the first thing up, so I won't have to sweat it out all night."

Since it was so difficult for Oprah to sit in her chair, she said she had to half lay in it all night. "The one moment I didn't," she told Lyn Tornabene, "was when they read the nominees and the camera was on me. It was the worst."

When Anjelica Huston's name was announced as the winner, Oprah says, "I was grateful to God that she won, because that dress was so tight I would not have been able

173

to walk up the seven steps to get it. As for my own loss, I didn't consider it a loss. I truly didn't consider it a loss. There was part of me that really wanted to win, and then there was another part of me, deep down inside, that didn't, because to have won the very first time out would have been too much for even me—too much, too soon. I like growing in stages, and I like the idea of developing as an actress and I want to become a great actress. I might not have had that same kind of drive if I had won the Oscar the first time out; my perception of who I am might have changed. And as it is, I still have some places to grow and something to look forward to. I mean, I just haven't paid enough acting dues."

When Lionel Richie appeared on Oprah's show he told her he thought she looked nervous at the Academy Awards. Oprah said, "I'm telling you, there aren't many black faces at the Oscars. So when you walk through the door, everybody looks around to see. 'Is it Lionel Richie? No. It's not Brenda Richie. Who is it? It's some black girl in a tight dress,' is what they say. And that's why I was so uncomfortable. I thought, 'Oh God! Lionel Richie is gonna see me in this dress!' It was the tightest dress known to womankind. It was a horrible night."

Of course, Oprah had another reason for being disappointed Oscar night. *The Color Purple* didn't receive one award. Oprah told Lyn Tornabene, "I could not go through the night pretending that it was okay that *Color Purple* did not win an Oscar. I was pissed and I was stunned."

Rather than attend any of the gala post-Oscar parties, such as the Governors' Ball, everyone who was present at the ceremony who had been associated with *The Color Purple* decided to assemble for a private party of their own. Slowly, the bitterness over not winning one single award began to fade as everyone present realized that winning an Academy Award wasn't their original goal in making *The Color Purple*, anyway. So what if it wasn't recognized at the Oscars? They knew they did their best. Each and every one of them was proud to have been part of the experience. Speaking for herself, Oprah said, "In retrospect, I think it's a greater statement that it won no awards than if it had won one or two. It put the whole Oscar in perspective for me, which is not to say I wouldn't want to win one now. It would be great, but it would never mean the same thing because for *The Color Purple* to be totally excluded says to me the Oscar isn't what I thought it was."

Oprah didn't waste any time putting the memory of her first Oscar night behind her. She had too many new experiences ahead to spend time worrying about something that was over. In the weeks ahead, she would begin work on her second feature film, *Native Son*. Her TV talk show, which had been retitled "The Oprah Winfrey Show," had been picked up for syndication and was scheduled to be broadcast nationally that fall. Oprah's big dreams were being realized—and she was loving every minute of it.

15

"Native Son"

"It's one of those times when a little voice tells me, 'Shut up.' "

"When we were Negroes we had to read this," Oprah told David Brenner on "Nightlife." She was discussing the novel *Native Son*, written in 1940 by Richard Wright. "It was required reading because it was a black book." Oprah, however, did not read the book until 1985, when she was cast to appear in a film version of it.

Native Son centers on Bigger Thomas, an impoverished young black man who, through a set of unusual circumstances, kills a wealthy white girl. "He commits a crime and then his mother has to beg for his life," explained Oprah.

Appearing on "Entertainment Tonight," Oprah described the film's message. "I think the essence of it is that we, society, create our own killers, our own menaces to the public, if we don't take responsibility, not only for ourselves, but for everybody else."

Unlike *The Color Purple*, which was filmed at a reported cost of $15 million, *Native Son* was budgeted for $2 million. In an effort to keep costs down, the cast, as well as the crew, worked for less than their regular salaries. Also appearing in the movie with Oprah were such well-known actors as Matt Dillon, Carroll Baker, and Geraldine Page. A relatively unknown actor, Victor Love, who had acting experience in theater and television, was cast to make his film debut as Bigger Thomas.

Carroll Baker told Judith Michaelson of *The Washington Post* that she received the script in London, where she was living. "As I flipped through it I got so involved . . ."

Geraldine Page agreed. She said, "Everyone who read this script was really excited by it."

During the filming of *Native Son*, a disagreement erupted between the director, Jerrold Freedman, and the film's producer, Diane Silver, over the direction of the story. In the novel, after Bigger Thomas kills the wealthy white girl, he proceeds to murder his girlfriend. This scene, to Jerrold Freedman's dismay, was not included in the film version. He told Aljean Harmetz of *The New York Times*, "The scene is pivotal in the novel because it underscores the disintegration of Bigger Thomas, a victim of racism and segregation in Chicago of the 1930s who in turn becomes a victimizer."

Defending the changes, Diane Silver said, "The angst that worked in the book was impossible to put on the screen. The book and this movie are about Bigger's realization that the depths of his fear are a reflection of his humanity."

Oprah's most dramatic moment in the movie takes place when her character, Mrs. Thomas, is forced to plead on bended knee to the murdered girl's mother for her own son's life. "Don't let them kill my boy. He's a poor boy, Miz Dalton. He ain't never had no chance. He's just a poor boy!

. . . Your peoples gonna move us outta our house and we ain't gonna have nowhere to live.'

"I remember the day we did that scene," Oprah said to David Brenner. "When you think of all the people who have experienced that . . ." Discussing the filming of the scene, Oprah revealed that she would force herself to hyperventilate just before she was scheduled to go on. It was a technique Steven Spielberg had taught her during the shooting of *The Color Purple*. Oprah said it had helped to anchor her in the moment. "Just the line where I say, 'Your people are gonna throw us out of our home and we ain't gonna have no place to live,' every time I got to that, I'd just break up, because the feeling of desperation, and being out on the street with her children . . . whew!"

When Oprah appeared on "Good Morning America," Barbara Walters said she thought Oprah's two film roles were similar and asked if she worried about being typecast. Oprah answered, "I remember in high school, when I was competing in drama, I used to do matriarchal figures all the time, Sojourner Truth and Harriet Tubman, characters like that. So it's just a crossover. I believe everything you do in your life prepares you for the moment which you're living now. So it makes sense that I would be doing this."

Some people criticized Oprah for her choice of film roles. A few even accused her of playing Aunt Jemima characters. "At first I would be very kind. Now I just want to slap them!" Oprah says.

Looking ahead to future film roles, Oprah revealed on "Entertainment Tonight" that she was ready to play a role with a woman who understands her sexuality. I keep playing all these old women with gray hair and stockings rolled up on their legs. I'm ready to cut loose, let loose, and let it go!"

When *Native Son* was released in December 1986, exactly one year after *The Color Purple*, it received tepid notices from film critics. In many of the reviews, however, Oprah was singled out for giving a moving performance. As early as August 1986, Oprah revealed she had an inkling all wouldn't be well for *Native Son*. She told Rick Du Brow of *The Los Angeles Times*, "It's one of those times when a little voice tells me, 'Shut up.'" After a few short weeks, due to poor box office response, *Native Son* was quietly pulled from theaters.

Although *Native Son* failed to perform well at the box office, some people speculated that Oprah might receive a second Academy Award nomination for her performance. When the nominees were announced, however, Oprah's name wasn't among them. She did make it back to the Oscars, though, this time as a presenter. She told the audience, "It's a lot easier on the nerves being a presenter than a nominee. You can concentrate on watching the show, instead of spending three hours making your deals with God promising to go on a diet, to go to church, to stop biting your nails, and to stay out of shopping malls and everything in between."

16

Syndication

"Syndication's going to make me a millionaire!"

"I want to be syndicated in every city known to mankind," Oprah said in 1985, shortly after making her first appearance on "The Tonight Show." There was just one hitch. WLS-TV had a firm contract with Oprah. If she were syndicated, WLS-TV would be unable to distribute the show because it was owned by ABC-TV. The FCC prohibits a network from syndicating its own programming to local stations on the grounds that it presents a conflict of interest. Eventually, a deal was worked out with King World Productions to distribute "The Oprah Winfrey Show," while WLS-TV would continue to produce it.

Oprah says six different companies bid for the rights to distribute her show. She went with King World Productions because it offered the best deal, a substantial share of the profits. King World Productions was also on a hot streak with two other programs it was distributing, which gave the company credibility.

Besides "The Oprah Winfrey Show," King World Productions' two biggest successes to date have been the syndicated versions of the "Wheel of Fortune" and "Jeopardy." Before King World began distributing "Wheel of Fortune" in 1983, it was considered a small, family-owned business, which operated out of Summit, New Jersey. For years, its primary source of revenue came from distributing episodes of "The Little Rascals" to local TV stations. Charlie King founded the company in the mid-sixties. When he died of a heart attack in 1973, his three sons, Michael, Bob, and Roger, took over the company. Under their helm, King World enjoyed moderate success, selling such game shows as "Tic Tac Dough" and "Joker's Wild" to local TV stations.

The story behind King World's acquiring the distribution rights to the nighttime syndicated "Wheel of Fortune" is indicative of the brothers' unique approach to business. Reportedly, Bob King was seated at the bar in the St. Regis Hotel in New York City discussing with a friend his desire to sell "Wheel of Fortune" to local TV stations. Seated nearby was Murray Schwartz, president of Merv Griffin Enterprises, which produces "Wheel of Fortune." Murray Schwartz told Jeff Pryor of *Electronics Media* magazine that it was obvious to him the two men were distributors of syndicated TV shows. Approaching Bob King, he introduced himself. "I gave him my card and the blood left his face. I said, 'If you're interested, you'll have to put up an advance of one million dollars.' "

The following week Bob King showed up at Murray Schwartz's Hollywood office with a crumpled check in his shirt pocket for one million dollars.

King World Productions sensed another hit in Oprah's TV talk show. Gathering tapes of Oprah's Chicago program,

King World showed them to various test groups across the country. The results strongly indicated that Oprah's appeal could easily carry over on a national level. During the test sessions, King World representatives also asked the focus groups to compare Oprah to Phil Donahue. "The thing I remember," Oprah told P. J. Bednarski in *Channels* magazine, "is that all the women said if they met Donahue, they'd be in awe. But if they met me, they'd ask me out to dinner." It's no wonder that King World pitched Oprah's show to TV stations as the perfect alternative to "Donahue."

"Oprah is the hottest-selling show I've ever had," Roger King told the *News American*. In all, a record-breaking 137 stations were scheduled to carry the newly syndicated "Oprah Winfrey Show."

Ironically, WJZ-TV in Baltimore was not among the stations that had acquired the rights to Oprah's show. Oprah had asked King World to let WJZ-TV get the first shot at bidding on her show, but a technical snag prevented the station from making an offer before another station, WMAR-TV, had already bought the rights. At Oprah's request, King World did offer first bidding to WJZ-TV's parent company, Group W, for its entire group of stations. But the bid Group W made for WJZ-TV was deemed too low by King World. WJZ-TV's program director, Jerry Eaton, said he wanted to make another bid for the station, independent of Group W, but it was too late. He told Bill Carter of *The Baltimore Sun*, "I feel like I was left out of the bidding. . . . We weren't dealt with fairly by the syndicator."

Questioned by Bill Carter about the situation, Roger King confirmed that Jerry Eaton was correct in maintaining that WJZ-TV wasn't given a chance to bid on Oprah's show. He said, "WJZ is a fine station, but I happen to have another client in Baltimore." WMAR was already running "Wheel of Fortune" and "Jeopardy." Roger King added that WMAR-TV's bid was hundreds of thousands dollars more than the one Group W made for WJZ-TV. He said the station "is paying a fortune for the show." Shortly after announcing that WMAR-TV had acquired the rights to carry "The Oprah Winfrey Show," Arnie Kleiner, the station's general manager, jokingly said he was so enthusiastic about the show that he planned to run it just before the eleven o'clock newscast. Instead, Oprah's show was scheduled directly opposite "People Are Talking."

Although disappointed that WJZ-TV wouldn't be carrying her show, Oprah said she wasn't troubled by WMAR-TV's decision to place her opposite her former co-host, Richard Sher. She told Bill Carter, "Richard does call and leave messages on my machine."

When asked for his response to the situation, Richard Sher told the *News American*, "I'm happy the way her program's gone over in Chicago. Oprah and I will remain good friends, but we'll beat her in the ratings. It will be an interesting battle." Richard Sher added that he felt his show had an advantage over Oprah's because it was local. "Oprah will not really be a part of the Baltimore community," he said.

Oprah, however, didn't believe it would make a difference with viewers where her show originated. As a matter of fact, with the exception of trying to omit local Chicago references, Oprah didn't plan to make any changes in the way her show was presented. She told *Family Circle*, "I have faith that the people in Tulsa and Nashville and New York are the same as they are in Chicago."

When Mike Wallace went to Chicago to interview Oprah for "60 Minutes," he observed that her staff was predominantly white and female. He asked if more blacks would be added to the staff once the show went national. Oprah answered, "I believe in excellence. And the people I have are excellent. I mean, it would be absolutely ridiculous to get rid of those people because they're white. That's racism in reverse. When we bring on additional staff, I will make sure that there's some black people included."

As for the staff consisting primarily of women, Debbie DiMaio said it was difficult to find men who could relate to the kinds of themes presented on "The Oprah Winfrey Show" because they're usually geared toward concerns that interest women.

Oprah wasn't the only personality with a TV talk show scheduled to premiere in the fall of 1986. Joan Rivers, David Brenner, Dick Cavett, and Jimmy Breslin were also entering the market with talk shows of their own. The difference was that Oprah's would be aired during the daytime. When asked what she thought the chances of her show enduring were, Oprah answered, "I think a show, any show, can endure as long as we are flexible and truthful. It won't endure if we start faking ideas or moments, or pretend that we're something we're not, or create an atmosphere that we believe people will buy into. Living on our guts seems to be the key, in addition to telling the truth. Television is the greatest medium in the world, and I think those of us who work in it are in a blessed position. We have a responsibility to enlighten, inform, and entertain, if we can. And as long as we do that, and do that with proof in mind, we won't fail. Success is about being honest, not only in your work, but in your life. And if you let that theory carry through in your work, then you have no problems."

Oprah understood that her biggest competition when she went national would more than likely be Phil Donahue's show. She found the prospect exciting. In a *U.S.A. Today* interview, Oprah said, "I'd love to go up against him head-to-head in all the markets at once! It would be so glorious to win!"

"I say Donahue's the king," Oprah told Rick Du Brow of *The Los Angeles Times*, "but I just want part of the kingdom."

"We're not out to wipe Donahue off the face of the earth, but it's plausible we'll knock him off the air," Stuart Hersch, chief operating officer of King World Productions, told *Savvy* magazine.

As part of the push to win station clearance for Oprah's show, King World pointed to her success in outrating Phil Donahue in Chicago. "They're building a whole piece of cloth out of one little thread," responded Janet Baser, research vice president of Multimedia, which distributed Phil Donahue's show.

The Donahue vs. Winfrey battle generated a lot of publicity in the national media, which was understandable. It was the first time the hugely successful Phil Donahue had what was considered a formidable competitor. The outcome of the battle was particularly intriguing. If Oprah did succeed in toppling Phil's talk-show kingdom, chances were good she could become an instant multimillionaire. In 1986, daytime shows drew an estimated $990 million in nonnetwork TV advertising, up from $263 million in 1975. Phil Donahue's high-rated talk show was partly responsible for the increase. If a station aired "Donahue," it was a sure bet viewers would stick around for further programming, such as the station's local newscast, which, compared with the profits it generates, is relatively inexpensive to produce. Is it any wonder that the local stations that had picked up Oprah's show were inviting a comparison between her and Phil Donahue as another incentive to pique the audience's interest?

"I have this fear they may promote me as the Second Coming," Oprah told Greg Bailey of *The Nashville Banner*. "The hype is used to get people to tune in. Once they do, they'll make up their own minds about me. They're not all going to love me."

The debut of "The Oprah Winfrey Show" in September 1986 would mark the first time a black woman hosted on her own a national TV talk show. As programming trends went, it couldn't have come at a better time. A black male, Bryant Gumbel, was hosting the number-one-rated network morning program, NBC-TV's "Today Show." In prime time, "The Cosby Show" was the country's most watched television program. It was quite a departure from

1957, when Nat King Cole couldn't even find a sponsor to carry his variety show.

Mike Wallace asked Oprah on "60 Minutes" how she'd react if her show didn't succeed nationally. "It'll do well," she responded. "If it doesn't, I will still do well. I will do well because I am not defined by the show. I think we are defined by the way we treat ourselves and the way we treat other people. It would be wonderful to be acclaimed as this talk-show host who's made it. That would be wonderful. But if that doesn't happen, there are other important things in my life."

The summer of 1986 brought two significant changes to Oprah's life. For starters, to celebrate the success of syndicating her talk show, Oprah moved into a bigger, more lavish apartment on the fifty-seventh floor of a high-rise with a very exclusive lakefront address. The apartment had once been owned by Evangeline Gouletas, a Chicago real-estate mogul and wife of former New York governor Hugh Carey, and was valued at more than $800,000.

Oprah told *Cosmopolitan*, "Evangeline left behind some nice touches—a wine cellar, a crystal chandelier lighting up the inside of my closet, and a marble bathtub with gold dolphins for spigots." The apartment also provided Oprah with a wraparound view of Chicago, including Lake Michigan.

Oprah said she bought the apartment as a gift to herself for accomplishing a goal she had set for herself, to become a millionaire by thirty-two. "I didn't break my promise. So I bought the apartment as my present."

The interior decorator Oprah hired to furnish her new home suggested to Oprah that she replace all her old furniture with newer pieces, so Oprah spent almost the entire summer with virtually nothing in the place but a bed.

Oprah also discovered love in the summer of 1986. His name was Stedman Graham and he headed a program called Athletes Against Drugs, which counseled young people on the dangers of drug abuse.

Stedman, a former model, had shared a passing acquaintance with Oprah because they were constantly running into each other at various Chicago social functions. He had asked her out for dinner, but Oprah turned him down. She was intimidated by his good looks and rationalized that he was up to no good. Some advice Oprah's mother had once given her kept ringing in her head. "Stay away from men who are prettier than you, or dumber," Vernita Lee warned. "They're either no good or after your money." But Stedman was determined to win a date with Oprah.

Each time he ran into Oprah, he would ask her. Each time Oprah would turn him down. Why? he'd ask. Oprah said her work schedule kept her too busy for a social life. Was she too busy to have lunch? Or cocktails? Still, Oprah refused his invitations.

Finally, Stedman caught Oprah on a day when her resistance was down. "It was at the end of a very rough, very long day," says Alice McGee, Oprah's press representative. A guest had canceled an appearance on the show. Plus, a tired and exhausted Oprah was expected to speak at a rally to drum up support for Hands Across America.

Just as Oprah was about to leave her office, she received a call from Stedman. He told her, "This is the last time I'm going to ask. Will you go out with me for dinner?"

Instead of dodging Stedman's invitation, Oprah surprised him by answering yes. What Stedman didn't realize was that Oprah was too tired to say no. As it turned out, it was a good thing for Oprah that she didn't refuse.

"I'm so glad I went!" she exclaimed to her coworkers the morning after their first date. "He bought me roses, paid for dinner, and was interested in what I had to say!"

Oprah agreed to see Stedman again, but told herself

they were "just friends." When Stedman was seen with Oprah at Hands Across America, Chicago newspaper columnists speculated that she might be falling in love. By summer's end, even Oprah was beginning to think it might be true, too.

"I think it's pretty serious," Oprah told Barbara Walters on "Good Morning America." "It's great fun. He's very kind and supportive."

When Barbara Walters reminded Oprah that she had once told her she didn't believe it was possible that she'd be meeting "Mr. Right," Oprah answered, "You're right. Up until seven or eight months ago, I said it would never happen. I have my career. I'll go on and live my life and that'll be fine.

"I think what happened is what I read about in all the women's magazines. They say if you stop looking you can find it."

Ironically, discussing the problem of meeting a suitable man, Oprah once told her audience, "This is what we've heard, 'You just really need to stop looking and putting pressure on it.' I've been told that. 'The minute you stop looking you will find him.' I've gone to many a banquet I didn't want to go to because I thought, 'Maybe he'll be here.' You walk into the room and you say, 'Okay, God, I'm not looking, but . . .?' "

Before meeting Stedman Graham, Oprah told Mike Wallace on "60 Minutes," "You know what I say to myself? If I lose forty pounds maybe it'll happen then. After the movie I said it would happen. Then before the Oscars. Now I don't know."

Calling Stedman "an overwhelmingly decent man," Oprah told *Ebony*, "He has made me realize a lot of the things that were missing in my life, like the sharing that goes on between two people."

When Oprah appeared on "The Late Show," with Joan Rivers, she described Stedman as "six feet six of terrific!"

"You wanna bring him out?" asked Joan.

"I don't know if he'll come," answered Oprah. "He's so private I don't think he will."

Joan Rivers tried to coax Stedman onstage, but he remained backstage. "I knew he wouldn't," commented Oprah. "And I respect that. Usually, you get guys when you're high profile who walk into a room and they're looking for a camera."

"It speaks highly of him that he didn't go on," says Alice McGee. "He doesn't want people to think of him as Mr. Oprah Winfrey."

When Joan Rivers observed that Oprah looked slimmer, Oprah credited her relationship with Stedman for being part of the reason. "It's helpful because he has such a great body," she said jokingly.

Taking a moment to discuss weight with Joan Rivers, Oprah reflected a new attitude about it. "I've reached a point in my life now where I think it's okay. I'm going to lose it. And you know what? The slower you lose it, the better. You know when you pig out and you fast and you pig out? You drop ten pounds in four days and it's back by the fifth? I'm done with that."

On the eve of her show going national, Oprah revealed to *Essence*, "I feel as good as you can feel and still live. Really, I mean, there are some days when I'm thinking, 'If it gets any better, I may just go jump over the moon.' "

17

"The Oprah Winfrey Show"

"People make fun of talk shows because we do transsexuals and their parents. But I feel if something is going on in the world and it's happening to somebody, maybe somebody else is interested in it. I really think you can do anything with good taste."

"**Y**ou know, there has been so much hoopla about this premiere show," Oprah told her audience in the first minute of her national debut, "that it's enough to give a girl hives. I've got 'em right now under my armpits."

Oprah's frankness came as no surprise. When asked by *USA Today* if the upcoming premiere of "The Oprah Winfrey Show" made her edgy, Oprah answered, "If I'm tense, I'll be open about it. I'll tell the audience, 'Hey, this is a pretty big deal!' "

Ironically, the debut of Oprah's national talk show on September 8, 1986, marked an anniversary for her. It was five years to the day that she had penned her suicide note back in Baltimore.

To build excitement and suspense, the topic of Oprah's first national show was kept secret. Chicago newspaper columnists speculated that Whoopi Goldberg or Steven Spielberg might make appearances. One columnist even suggested that Michael Jackson might be Oprah's first guest. "I've been very busy these last few weeks traveling to as many of your cities as possible to introduce myself," Oprah said. "And in every new town people would ask, 'Oprah, who are the guests for the first show? Is it Mother Teresa? The Pope? Greta Garbo?'

"We decided to do what we do best and that is a show about and with everyday people. I've been doing talk shows now for years and one thing I've learned is that, no matter how far down you go, and I tell you, I've been down on my knees with the best of you, no matter how low you feel, this show always allows people, hopefully, to understand the power they have to change their own lives. If there's one thread running through each show we do it is the message that you are not alone. And if you feel you are alone today's show may change that.

"I don't have a lot of problems in my life, I have to tell you. Things are going pretty good for me right now. But two things have bugged me for years. The first, my thighs. The second, my love life. It was not a happy day when I found out about the Yale University study saying that women not married by the age of 40 have a greater chance of being killed by a terrorist than walking down the aisle to say, 'I do.' I tell you, I wore a black armband for a week mourning that one," Oprah commented as her audience laughed in appreciation. She then went on to introduce her guests, which included an author who had written a book, which sold for $95, on how to snare a mate and some people who had bought the book and tested its methods.

That same day, Phil Donahue televised his show from Los

191

Angeles. A third of the cities that had picked up Oprah's show were airing it opposite "Donahue." Los Angeles was one of them. Phil's guest that afternoon was the Mayflower Madam, Sidney Biddle Barrows. Later that day, both Oprah and Phil appeared on their Los Angeles stations' respective newscasts. Referring to Phil's presence in Los Angeles, Oprah jokingly said, "You gotta go home sometime, Phil!"

Meanwhile, in Baltimore, to combat the premiere of Oprah's show, "People Are Talking" featured an interview Richard Scher had taped earlier with Lucille Ball. His studio guest was Jim Harris, son of convicted killer Jean Harris.

Besides Los Angeles and Baltimore, Oprah's show premiered in 136 other cities, an unprecedented number for a new syndicated TV program. Oprah realized that a great deal of attention would be focused on her first show and had expressed a desire that she not be judged solely by it. "It's just not gonna be a normal day for us," she said. As it turned out, the general response to Oprah, if not necessarily to her first show, was enthusiastic.

"A lot of people didn't know what to expect, but all the response we've gotten so far has been very positive," Jack Mazzie, vice president and general manager of WEEK-TV, a Peoria, Illinois, station, told Robert Feder of *The Chicago Sun-Times*. He added that viewers thought Oprah was "bouncy, full of life, very vital, and extremely intelligent."

Bill Carter, TV critic for *The Baltimore Sun*, wrote, "She brings expansive energy and spontaneous enthusiasm to this tired format, while leaving out the pseudo-intellectual bilge that has turned the previous talk-show giant, Phil Donahue, into a pretentious bore."

USA Today described Oprah as "a throw-your-arms-around-'em talk-monger who hopes to dethrone Phil Donahue as ruler of the daytime talkies."

Bill Mann of *The Oakland Tribune* wrote, "What sharply differentiates Winfrey from her talk-show rivals is her down-home, almost funky style. . . . Oprah isn't so full of herself that she'll avoid asking the question most viewers would like to ask."

Time magazine wrote, "An an interviewer, Winfrey lacks Donahue's pungency. But she compensates with an earthy spontaneity, personal involvement, and a knack for making guests and viewers feel comfortable."

Not every review was favorable, of course.

Howard Rosenberg of *The Los Angeles Times* wrote, "If initial episodes are a sample, 'Oprah Winfrey' is little more than a low-brow 'Donahue.' . . . She is less articulate, cerebral, and polished than Donahue, but more explosive and unpredictable."

Steve McKerrow of *The Baltimore Evening Sun:* "From its topic—how to find and hook a mate—to Winfrey's pouncing like a schoolteacher upon audience members who might have nodded their head in agreement with a guest, the show could just as easily have been any edition of 'Donahue' of the last decade or so."

Lewis Grossberger wrote in *Rolling Stone,* " 'The Oprah Winfrey Show,' the one new daytime talkie, is like watching 'Donahue' with an imposter playing the role of Phil. The two shows are exactly the same: wandering host, smug experts, glum victims, jump-right-in audience, and all that endless jabbering about problems, problems, problems. Divorced transvestites. Overweight claustrophobics. Schizophrenic stepchildren of hearing-impaired Satan worshipers . . ."

When Oprah appeared on "Nightlife" with David Brenner, he kidded her about some of the guests that have appeared on her show. "I saw transsexual parents, gay bashers," said David Brenner.

"People make fun of talk shows because we do transsexuals and their parents," Oprah responded. "But I feel if something is going on in the world and it's happening to somebody, maybe somebody else is interested in it. I really think you can do anything with good taste."

"Let me just say this," Oprah added later, "because talk shows get a bad rap, all the time, about doing these sensational things. But we also do some incredible shows that make a difference in people's lives. We did a show with children of divorced parents, with children crying, because it was the first chance they had had to express their feelings about it. We did a show with people who were terminally ill and won't be around six weeks from now. We did a show with women who had been dumped by their husbands. . . . With all the poking fun of it and everything, which I know critics like to do, but to the people that these things happen to, it's very serious."

When Oprah appeared on "The Late Show" with Joan Rivers, the two discussed their feelings about receiving what they felt was unfair press. "Isn't it painful?" Oprah asked. "It's like they don't regard what the people think, what the people say, what the people watch. I think it's the worst."

Oprah conceded that, for the most part, she received good press, but added, "There are times when some little obscure magazine, or some little obscure gossip page will say some horrible things about you."

In an interview in *Essence* magazine, Oprah discussed a particular kind of criticism she has received from some blacks. "You'll get a group of sisters who say, 'Well, she don't look like nothing. I don't see how she did it.' And now I get calls from people who say to me, 'You know, you hug the white people [on your show] more than you hug the black people,' things like that. It's unfortunate, because sometimes I feel that some black people really don't want you to succeed. Some don't want you to go on the air and just be yourself. They want a civil rights movement every morning."

An article in the *Village Voice*, written by a black writer, accused Oprah of being a "black mammy" for white people. "I think that's ridiculous," says Oprah's Tennessee State University speech teacher, Dr. Jamie Williams. "Oprah doesn't behave at all like a black mammy. Oprah behaves like a sensitive human being. When we expect every person in our race to be a crusader, we are expecting what is not a normal kind of thing.

"It would seem to me that you would have to give Oprah time. She is thirty-three, that's not forty-three. She has just gotten to the top of the ladder. When you first get there you have to get your bearings. I would say that some of the things that people are expecting of her may very well come in time. If they don't, that's still her life to live the way she sees it. She is a highly successful black woman. I have never heard her say anything that would suggest to me that she doesn't realize she's black. I don't know what all the hue and cry is about. Too often we want to criticize and carp about people because they're not conforming to some kind of preconceived notion that we have about them. Personally, I don't think we have the right."

To appease some of the viewers who had written to her voicing their dislike, Oprah took some of them out to lunch. "All people who had written me letters saying what a —— I was," she told Joan Rivers, "I took them all to lunch. So, five bottles of champagne later, I still had people who were hostile. I was so depressed because there was this one lady who said, 'You know, I don't like the way you wear your hair. I don't like your earrings. I don't like your clothes. I don't like the way you talk to people. You think you're such hot stuff. I'm telling you, I don't like you no way.' "

Laughing about it, Oprah said, "The thing about it is, you get a hundred letters from people who say you're wonderful. And then you get the one . . ."

As a word of advice to rising stars, she added, "If you go to open the letter, and there's no return address on the outside, bad sign. Bad! Don't open it. It'll ruin your day."

According to the A. C. Nielsen Company's ratings, posted three months after "The Oprah Winfrey Show's" national debut, it was obvious Oprah had little reason to worry about a smattering of isolated, negative mail. In every one of the country's ten largest cities, "The Oprah Winfrey Show" was the number-one-rated program in its slot.

"This is an absolutely historic moment in television syndication," Moira Dunlevy, vice president of research for King World Productions, told Robert Feder in *The Chicago Sun-Times*. "Never has any first-run, syndicated show of any kind opened so strongly right out of the gate."

WABC-TV, the New York station that carries "The Oprah Winfrey Show," was so impressed by its high ratings that it decided to move the show out of its morning time slot and into a more competitive afternoon slot, directly leading into its afternoon newscast and opposite—who else?—Phil Donahue.

Despite her success, Oprah told "Entertainment Tonight," "People don't treat me like I'm a star, or a celebrity. They treat me like I'm one of them. People say to me, 'Wait here. I'm going to get a pencil,' unlike with stars, who they'll say to, you know, 'Excuse me, Mr. Peck? May I please have your autograph?' With me, it's 'wait here.' "

Of course, with the phenomenal success of "The Oprah Winfrey Show," Oprah differed from her audience in a very significant way. In December 1986, *Variety* reported that Oprah could become the highest-paid performer in show business, earning more money than even Johnny Carson or Bill Cosby. It was estimated her salary could reach as high as $31 million. According to the report, by 1988 "The Oprah Winfrey Show" was expected to have earned an estimated $125 million. Allegedly, the deal Oprah's lawyer negotiated for her with King World Productions gave her "25 percent of the gross right off the top." When asked by *TV Guide* to confirm the report, a representative for Oprah declined to answer. The most sensational quote Oprah has made, to date, regarding her income was one published in *People* magazine. According to *People*, she said, in January 1987, "I have allotted myself to personally spend only $1 million this year. That's how much I'm giving myself to play with."

A syndication executive, who demanded anonymity, told Lloyd Shearer of *Parade* magazine, "At this point, Oprah's talk show is carried by 135 TV stations, and she's in demand. But estimates of her fortune are highly exaggerated. I'd say she's worth between $3 million and $4 million."

"I feel so fulfilled," Oprah told Barbara Walters on "Good Morning America." "The great thing about attaining some level of success in your life is being spiritually in a place where you accept it and feel good about it and know why you are there, and not be afraid that tomorrow it's going to end. People always say, 'What about tomorrow?' I'm very pleased to say that I live for today, and enjoy today. I really don't expect any of this to stay the same. Hopefully, we all continue to grow and it gets better. And you go on to another place."

Looking ahead, Oprah told *Adweek* that she had founded her own production company, which she named Harpo (Oprah spelled backwards). Oprah said she wanted to use the company to develop future TV and movie projects. "Most people start companies to make money. Right now, as it is, I make a lot of money and you can only buy so many towels and so many houses. Money is not the issue."

Oprah's success has also enabled her to provide lavish gifts for family and friends. Last year she purchased a condominium for her mother. It's also not unusual for Oprah to surprise relatives and friends by presenting them with a mink coat. Her cousin Jo Baldwin, vice president of Harpo, Inc., told *Ebony*, "Oprah is generous to a fault."

"I will do the kind of work that even if I didn't get paid to do it, I would still feel that it was important to do."

In the spring of 1987, one of Oprah's top priorities was taping a situation comedy pilot for ABC-TV. Stuart Bloomberg, vice president for comedy-and-variety-series development, told Louis Chunovic of the *Hollywood Reporter*, "We have a concept [in which] she would play a character similar to herself, [who] has a talk show. . . . The series would start when the show ends. It's about her life as a single woman trying to do a daily show, about her office staff and her personal life."

Oprah made it clear that the prime-time series wouldn't interfere with her duties as a talk-show host. "At this point, while we're waiting to gear up, I actually feel rather bored. I feel like there's ten hours after my show each day to do something."

As for the direction she planned to take with her personal life, Oprah said, "I try to move with the flow of life and not to dictate what life should be for me, but just let it flow. So there may be a husband and there may be children. There may not be. I will celebrate either course that life hands me."

When asked to describe what she thought her friends might say about her behind her back, Oprah answered, "My friends would probably say I need to be more organized. But I say that, too. They would say I'm very unconventional. Some people don't know how to take me sometimes. But I'm honest. I really am. I do just what I feel and hope it works."

18
Oprah, Studio Mogul

"The fact it even got built is the most astounding thing to me."

"**T**hat pilot was a C if anything. An average bore," Oprah explained to a reporter who inquired about her proposed sitcom series in 1988. "I knew when I saw the script, but by then it was all scheduled, and I found it hard to say no. In this business a man who says no is seen as assertive and in control, but a woman is a bitch. So I went ahead. But for now, I'm shelving the sitcom idea forever— temporarily. I want to do great work, and five years from now I want to be seen as not only a great actress but as a successful businesswoman."

Oprah's first coup as a businesswoman was obtaining ownership and control of her TV-talk show from ABC-TV in the summer of 1988. She credited her lawyer and business adviser, Jeffrey Jacobs, with being instrumental in making the deal happen. In fact, it was Jacobs who first approached Oprah with the idea of assuming control over her television series. At the time, she had difficulty embracing the concept. "My vision of control was not having people tell me what to do," she explained. "I was still thinking like a slave. You have to go to another level of thinking to say, 'I want to own it.'"

The news that she had acquired ownership of her talk show was delivered to Oprah while she was in Los Angeles, taping commercials promoting her show. "I was in my room at the Bel-Air Hotel," she recalled, "killing flies because I left the window open. I had a towel and was swinging it around the room when Jeff came in and told me that we got ownership of the show." Jacobs sat down with Oprah and explained the specifics of the deal, but she was too stunned to absorb the information. Moments after he left her room, however, it finally dawned on Oprah what had transpired. "When it hit me I went screaming down the hall," she revealed. Alarmed by Oprah's screams, Jacobs quickly returned to check on her. "He thought something terrible had happened!"

A short while later, Oprah was still having trouble fully adjusting to the implications of owning her series. "You sit and it's very difficult at the time to see what it really means. For me, I started thinking about my history. I started thinking about what this means as a female, as a black female, about where I come from, how did this happen to me, my growing up in Mississippi and I still don't understand all that it really means. I guess it could blow your mind ... I do know that it means the ceiling is lifted.

"Freedom is a very difficult concept. All of your life, you think if you draw a salary, you'll do okay. It's difficult to think in terms of unlimited possibilities. I've said I want to do great plays, great movies, great shows for myself and other people—and now there is absolutely no excuse not to do it."

Earlier that year, Oprah had successfully completed co-producing her first television mini-series, "The Women of Brewster Place," based on a novel by Gloria Naylor. She first came across the book while filming *The Color Purple* and was determined to see it produced. When every major American television network passed on the idea, Oprah arranged to meet personally with executives from ABC television to try and change their minds. At that meeting she handed out copies of the book.

"Look," Oprah told the stunned executives, "the reason you passed on this the first time is because none of you has read it. So I want everyone to read it, and I'll call you on Tuesday." By Tuesday, a deal was made. In addition to serving as co-producer, Oprah was also signed to play the lead character, Mattie Michael.

When filming on the mini-series began in Los Angeles in the spring of 1988, Oprah was accompanied by several key members from her staff who understood they were in Hollywood to learn how a dramatic television series was made. "They had the lowliest positions," said Oprah. "You know, production assistants, running around learning, learning, learning, working with the director one week, with accounting, with the art department. It was a learning tree for all of us."

"The Women of Brewster Place" chronicled the lives of seven women living on an impoverished street. There were no lead male roles. Realizing this would draw added attention on her project Oprah said, "Because we were all females, I didn't want to create any kind of friction so that it could ever be said that women can't get along. I was very conscious of being on the set before everybody else was. If I was supposed to be dressed at a certain time, I was dressed ten minutes earlier."

Following completion of "The Women of Brewster Place," Oprah returned to Chicago, where she continued to tape her daily TV-talk show. Shortly after acquiring control of her series, Oprah was in the news again with the announcement that she had purchased her own 88,000 square foot studio and production facility in Chicago for an estimated $10 million. Besides housing "The Oprah Winfrey Show," Oprah hoped Hollywood producers would be interested in utilizing her Chicago-based production complex. "I want people to know that there is a great state-of-the-art production house here that you can use for considerably less money than you can anywhere else," she told the press. "Whatever we do here will be good work, and good work will follow us. Other people will be attracted to this studio because of that."

With Harpo Productions, Oprah's company, becoming more viable, Oprah decided it was time to sit down with her staff to discuss the immediate future. She told them, "This is new for me, new for all of us. You have to move up to another level of thinking, which is true for me and everybody else here. Everybody has to learn to think differently, (to think) bigger, to be open to the possibilities."

Discussing her staff, which totalled seventeen in 1988, with *The Hollywood Reporter*, Oprah said, "I'm building a family here. I hire people with the intention of letting them move up and grow into being everything they can be, from the receptionist onwards. If you can do it, I want you to do it. I haven't had any management courses, but I think fairness is the best management there is. If you treat people fairly, they understand that you have their best interests at heart and they work for you. They'll do anything for you. For all the people who said it can't be done—we're doing it. I'm involved in everything here. I pick the juices for the refrigerator, I decide what popcorn we're going to use and I sign every check. I hire people who are very good at what they do and I let them do it. You excel, they excel and everything runs very smoothly. It's all setting priorities, knowing how to create a balance in your life. It's about balance."

Shortly after gaining control of her series, Oprah was told by various people that the special relationship she shared with her staff would more than likely change for the worse. "Everybody tells me that you cannot have true friendships with people whose salaries you control," stated Oprah, "but I just don't think that's true in my case. Because they were my friends before I signed their paychecks. We sort of all grew up together with this show. Like, they were there, ya' know—when all this happened."

Gaining control of her professional life wasn't the only thing Oprah was interested in during the summer of 1988. With her career reaching new heights, Oprah decided it was finally time to do something about her weight. Meeting with a doctor, she arranged to go on a liquid diet for six weeks. "Every day I mixed my little protein pack— this Optifast—in my little Opticup, measured six inches, poured some water in it, shook it up and no matter where I was, that was breakfast, lunch and dinner," recalled Oprah. She also initiated an exercise routine. "I started walking a mile a day, adding a half a mile, adding another half a mile until I was up to six and a half miles running," she said, "and I did this every day."

In an attempt to understand why she overate, Oprah kept a journal. She shared an entry from it with viewers on her television show. "The behavior psychologist who meets with you before the diet—and once a week during— said to me that I have got to make this bigger than weight because obviously the fat itself is not enough to make me want to lose it. So what is the bigger issue here?

"Self-esteem. For me, it is getting control of my life. I realize that this fat is a blocker. It is like having mud in my wings. It keeps me from flying.

"It is both comfortable and uncomfortable for me to walk into a room with people I don't know. My fat puts them at ease, make them less threatened, makes me insecure. My insecurity makes them comfortable. So I dream of walking into a room one day when this fat is not the issue. That will happen this year because the bigger issue is going to be making myself the best I can be."

A revelation about why she overate came to Oprah shortly after beginning her diet. It involved her longtime boyfriend, Stedman Graham. They had just returned to Oprah's apartment after seeing a movie together. Although Oprah was hoping to have Stedman's complete attention, he chose to spend the time playing a video game. Disappointed, Oprah thought to herself, "I've got to eat!" She headed for the kitchen and then stopped herself. "Why do I feel this way?" she wondered. "A minute ago I wasn't hungry. I'd been through the whole movie, resisted all that popcorn and candy." Her confusion cleared when she suddenly realized she was feeling anxious because she wasn't getting the attention she desired from Stedman. "That's when I realized it was a pattern," she told readers of *Essence* magazine. "I saw that when I had any kind of anxiety in my life, I would instantly want to eat. All those years when I said, 'I'm just eating because I like food.' All those years when I said, 'I never have stress in my life! I don't know what stress is!' I didn't have it because I blocked the stress by eating."

Oprah began to understand she turned to food as a way of dealing with a life she felt was out of control. Looking around her apartment, she noticed it was a mess. Her car was a mess. Her work was a mess. Putting together a story for her show that would normally take thirty minutes, took hours. "My whole life was jumbled, and the extra weight became a shield that I could hide behind as well as an excuse I could fall back on."

During her diet, there were a couple of occasions when Oprah freely admits she slipped. A vacation in Hawaii with Stedman served as the catalyst for one slip. Seeing that the change in routine was making Oprah agitated, Stedman said to her, "Why don't you just decide you're going to eat on vacation and not make yourself crazy? When you go home you can start the diet again." Warming up to Stedman's suggestion, Oprah decided to go one better and asked, "How about if I just had one cheeseburger and got it out of my system?" To which Stedman replied, "Are you crazy?" For the rest of the afternoon, Oprah was obsessed with satisfying her craving for a cheesburger. "I thought if I didn't have a cheeseburger I was going to die," she said. When Stedman finally left the hotel room for a golf lesson, Oprah quickly seized upon the opportunity. She opened every window in their hotel room and then ordered a bacon-avocado cheeseburger. "It was the best I ever had," she recalled, relishing the memory. That night, Oprah made up for her slip by running an extra mile on the golf course. "I was able to get back on track before I did any real damage," she explained.

A frozen halibut tucked away in her freezer at home later became a target of Oprah's obsession with food. "I remember leaving the office once because I had become fixated on that halibut," she said. "I was going to go home and microwave it." By the time Oprah arrived at home, however, she instead decided to phone her food counsellor. "I remember standing in my bathroom and feeling like an addict over that frozen halibut. It was that day I decided that I was no different from an addict."

By November, Oprah had succeeded in losing sixty-seven pounds. Displaying her new svelte figure for the first time on her television show, Oprah pulled on sixty-seven pounds of animal fat in a wagon. She told her viewers, "This is what sixty-seven pounds of fat looks like. I can't lift it, but I used to carry it around every day. And when you talk about making yourself the best you can be, I'm glad I did this for my heart because my poor heart had to send blood to all of this."

Responding to the rumor she lost the weight for Stedman, Oprah said, "I love Stedman very much and he cares about me and has been very supportive of me—fat and thin—(But) I did not do this for Stedman, and anybody who is overweight and whose spouse or friends are telling you to do it, you know you cannot do it for anybody but yourself."

Phoning Oprah live on the air, Stedman told her, "I have so much respect for you as a person for losing the weight ... Our relationship is one thing, but the respect I have for you as a person being able to acquire that much discipline is one of the most amazing things that I have ever experienced. I saw a diamond in the rough ... I said that you have a lot of potential, you have a great body and you have great curves. You're attractive and you just need to streamline it."

At the conclusion of the show Oprah told her viewers, "Every day for the rest of my life is going to be a struggle not to succumb once more to the old buffet table. And I am by no means through. It, for me, as I said earlier, was a means of getting my life under control."

Losing the weight, Oprah noticed that people responded to her differently. "You would not believe how different it is," she told Us magazine. "It is amazing to me. There's a validation you get in somebody's eyes as a thin person. There's something about being overweight that whatever you say, whatever your impressions are about a given subject, they just don't mean as much. It's not even a conscious thing, I don't think. I don't think people realize it, but I see it, and I feel it."

The drawback of Oprah's highly-publicized diet was the subsequent attention she received every time she ate in public. Citing a skiing trip she went on soon after her weight loss, Oprah said she was in a restaurant one morning debating whether or not to order two strips of bacon. "I remember trying to decide, 'Do I get the bacon or not?

Because if I get the bacon, I'm gonna hear about it.' I got the bacon, but I didn't even eat it. But a guy came over to me and he said, 'What are you doing with that bacon? You shouldn't be eating that!'

"I was in a restaurant with my staff one night," she continued, "I was not eating anything and it was printed in the paper the next day that I was popping shrimps down like popcorn. What offended me was that I didn't eat anything. If I had been doing that, I would have expected that to be printed. Two days later, the waiter called the paper and said he didn't serve me anything, so I was vindicated. That's why I stopped going to my diet classes. I started out in the main sessions like everyone else, eighteen fat people sitting in a circle. But everything *I* said got printed in the paper."

A year after publicizing her weight loss on her television show, Oprah had regained approximately twelve pounds. Discussing the added weight with *USA Today* Oprah said, "I'm never going to diet again. I'm going to practice what I preach, that when you're struggling against the grain you're going in the wrong direction ... I've been a professional dieter for thirteen years and I'm still struggling." Oprah was reluctant to elaborate further on the issue "because I know everything I say will become a tabloid headline, but I've decided not to let food control my life any more. I intend to live like a thin person, and if I want mashed potatoes, I'll have it. And I have started to lose (the) weight."

The tabloids' hysterical coverage of Oprah's subsequent weight gain was, understandably, a sensitive issue for her. "Every time I saw something printed in the tabloids, I'd just cringe," she revealed. A funny thing, however, happened recently when Oprah picked up a paper with the headline, "OPRAH WINFREY DIET DISASTER!". "I remember a time I would have just been destroyed," said Oprah. "I would have felt that I let America down—that everybody who is dieting now is going to think I'm a failure and that people are going to quit because of me. But for the first time, I looked at it, I read it, and I moved on. I never thought another thing about it. For the first time. Now I know I'm growing up."

Oprah's new-found resilience towards the tabloids would be severely tested in the spring of 1990 when the *National Enquirer* ran an exclusive interview with Oprah's half-sister, Patricia Lloyd. In the article Patricia charged that Oprah was pregnant at the age of fourteen. According to Patricia, the baby was born prematurely and died shortly afterwards.

Shortly after the article appeared, Oprah responded by issuing a statement to *Parade* magazine that said, "It saddens me deeply that a publication would pay large sums of money to a drug-dependent, deeply disturbed individual and then publish her remarks. My heart goes out to my half-sister, who is obviously in a lot of pain. Truth has been the foundation of my adult life, and I have always told the truth about my childhood—which, as I have said many times, was unfortunately very troubled and confusing.

"It is true that when I was fourteen years old, I became pregnant. The baby was born prematurely and died shortly after birth. The experience was the most emotional, confusing and traumatic of my young life. I had hoped that this matter could stay private until I was fully able to deal with my own deep emotions and feelings, so that I could share this experience in a way that could best help educate other young girls who are trying to cope with all the ramifications of sexual abuse."

Oprah's four-year relationship with Stedman Graham has been a constant source of speculation for the tabloids since she emerged as a national celebrity in 1986. She told *Essence* magazine it's been the most difficult issue they've had to face in their relationship. "But we've been getting tougher skins," she added.

Responding to the often-asked question, "When are you and Stedman going to marry?" Oprah told *TV Guide* in 1990, "You know, everybody wants me to get married! Not because people are truly interested in my happiness ... They want to see a wedding! They want a wedding! And I'm gonna give them a wedding—when I'm ready."

Recently, it dawned on Oprah that she had gotten "caught up in all the pressure about getting married, and that I'm not really interested in marriage right now. I'm not ready. I think it would be unfair to put us in this position." Referring to the demands she faces daily in her career, Oprah added, "I can't do all this and be a wife, too. Stedman knows it and I know it. And Stedman said it was the most mature thing he'd ever heard me say.

"Because I can't even get home on time, or keep Raisin Bran in the cupboard, I'm not prepared to be there for somebody."

The success of Oprah's mini-series, "The Women of Brewster Place," prompted ABC to approach her about developing a prime-time series centered around the character she played, Mattie Michael. Oprah welcomed the opportunity to star in the series, which would be filmed at her production facility in Chicago, because it would show television viewers a side of black people they weren't normally used to seeing. "Most people out there have no contact with black people," said Oprah. "Their only images are the ones portrayed on television ... There's a whole reality outside of what people know, where the black community functions on its own, where people own businesses, where people care about property and their children and pay their taxes ... The point of having your own company is that you can show that."

"Brewster Place" premiered as a half-hour series on ABC television in May, 1990. Before the series had a chance to build its audience, ABC had decided against renewing it for the fall. Shortly before "Brewster Place" premiered,

Oprah told *USA Today*, "I'm very hopeful, but if it doesen't work I won't have the if-I'd-onlys, not at all. First, 'The Oprah Winfrey Show' is still my bosom, my root and my foundation. Without it, nothing else could happen. And I believe that when we finish thirteen episodes, I can say I gave it everything, and that will be the truth."

Four years after premiering nationally in America, "The Oprah Winfrey Show" continued to be the top-ranked syndicated talk show. In 1989 Channel 4 began carrying Oprah's talk show. Following Oprah's enthusiastic reception on BBC's "Wogan", English station owners who carried "The Oprah Winfrey Show" were confident she'd be an immediate hit. So far, the popularity of her show has surpassed their expectations, but not her's. She's not in the least surprised by her UK success, stating, "The subjects, whether in the US or England, aren't that different because I think people are the same wherever you go.

"If your husband is having an affair, it's just as painful if you're in London or Los Angeles. For the things that really count in life, people are all the same, despite different cultural backgrounds."

When a reporter asked Oprah if her success has lived up to her own expectations, she answered, "It's all that it's cracked up to be and more, and not because of the money, the studio, the attention. What people don't recognize about my life is my peace. I have such peace—and there is no price to pay for that. My lack of anxiety and insecurity comes from that. My life is far better than it appears to be because of the pleasure and joy that comes from inner peace. You don't know what peace I have in my life—there's no way that anybody can know that."

19

Passages

"Think like a queen. A queen is not afraid to fail. Failure is another stepping-stone to greatness."

"**S**o why aren't we married?" a playful Oprah toyingly asked a reporter, anticipating his next question regarding her long-standing relationship with Stedman. "A good question," she good-naturedly responded, and then added, "but one with many answers. The obvious is . . . I can be impossible to live with because I am so controlling. And I'm the worst with Stedman because I know he won't leave me. Sometimes I think I'm testing him and he passes every test by letting me be.

"Then, too, there is the question of whether I really wanted to get married, or whether I feel I should because society expects that of me. Frankly, a piece of paper legalizing what Stedman and I have together couldn't make it any better than it already is. So, unless we decided to have children, it wouldn't bother me if we never got married."

But on Friday afternoon, October 10, 1992, Oprah was confronted with a life-changing surprise that caught her completely off-guard. She was spending the afternoon with her close friend, TV-news anchorwoman, Gayle King Bumpus, at the farmhouse she had recently purchased on 160-acres of land in Indiana. Gayle was in town for the weekend and the two longtime friends were visiting in the kitchen. Stedman was due to arrive any minute with a copy of a forthcoming "Oprah Winfrey Show" they intended to view. An unexpected change in plans, however, prevented them from viewing the tape—at least on that weekend. Hearing Stedman pull up, Oprah walked outside to meet him. In less than a minute's time, she returned to the kitchen with surprising news. Looking at Gayle, a dazed yet excited Oprah said, "You are not going to believe this. Stedman just proposed!"

The proposal was made quickly, and without fanfare, causing Oprah to wonder if she even heard Stedman correctly. "Is this a proposal?" she asked him. "I want you to marry me," he answered directly. "I think it's time." Mulling the idea over, Oprah nonchalantly responded, "Ah, that's really great."

Over the course of the next four weeks, Oprah and Stedman broke the news of their engagement to several close friends, with a request that they keep it under wraps. However, on Thursday, November 6, Oprah went public with her announcement. She was making a guest appearance on Gayle's news program, which aired on Hartford, Conn. TV-station WFSB, and the conversation suddenly turned personal. "Shall we talk about husbands and marriage?" Gayle asked Oprah. "Well," Oprah responded, without missing a beat, as she addressed the viewing audience, "Gayle was there the weekend that Stedman proposed."

Although Oprah's appearance was on a local news

program, details of her engagement were broadcast nationally within hours. In fact, the news spread so quickly that Oprah didn't even have a chance to call her father Vernon in Nashville to personally tell him that she and Stedman were engaged.

With the engagement now public knowledge, there was intense speculation regarding why Stedman had finally decided to propose. Several of Oprah's friends suspected that she was anxious to marry because, as she neared forty, the opportunity to have children would become increasingly more difficult. Giving credence to this speculation was a comment Oprah had recently made regarding children. "I would never have children without the benefit of marriage," she told a reporter, adding, "the benefit for them—as I recall all too well what it is like to be an illegitimate child. Also, with a child, but without a marriage, how could I speak before the thousands of teenagers I address each year and advise them not to bear children unless they are married? It doesn't matter that I am near forty and can well afford to take care of a hundred as easily as one child without a husband. I would still feel the hypocrite."

Yet, at the same time, Oprah remained ambivalent about the prospect of having children—even after news of her engagement was made public. "Do I want to have a child of my own?" she asked rhetorically. "Sometimes I think, yes, I do want to have that experience, and other times I must admit having a child is not a deep yearning at this time. Maybe I am afraid. Raising a child is such a serious business. You have to be emotionally mature and responsible and I'm not sure I'm describing me when I say that, at least not yet. But I'm getting there."

Hollywood casting director Reuben Cannon, who had become a close friend of Oprah's when they worked on *The Color Purple*, dismissed the speculation about Oprah's desire to marry so she could have children and offered his own theory to *People* magazine regarding why his famous friend

213

was making plans to marry. He believed that it was simply a matter of timing for Oprah. "She doesn't do anything under pressure," he said. "She trusts her spiritually guided instincts. She knows exactly what she needs at a certain time."

Although Oprah and Stedman had become officially engaged, they didn't share an exact wedding date with the public. Initially, they told friends they'd be married "sometime in '93." But as 1994 approached, Oprah and Stedman distanced themselves even further from committing to an exact date—at least publicly.

As expected, there were reports in the media that the date had been set and then postponed. With a nod to the tabloids, Oprah said, "I have never set a date for the wedding. It's because of the tabloids that there's been a public perception that the wedding has been on and off."

Oprah also chose not to sport an engagement ring because she doesn't like rings. "If you've noticed or watched over the years," she told viewers on her show, "I don't wear rings. I've only ever wanted one ring [a wedding ring]."

Even though Stedman popped the question, close friends of the couple were split down the middle over who was responsible for not setting an actual wedding date. "He's a proud man and he is marriage shy," offered Chicago anchorwoman Robin Robinson, who was romantically linked to Stedman in the early eighties. They became involved several years after Stedman's divorce from his first wife, Glenda, and she believed it affected his desire to become a husband for the second time. "The general ill-informed opinion is that Oprah didn't want to marry him. I would question that speculation. He was hurt by his first marriage not working out, and he doesn't like making mistakes."

However, while discussing their engagement with a reporter, Oprah admitted that she still had her own misgivings about marriage. "It does scare me a little bit, the whole idea of being married to somebody for the rest of your life," she revealed. "You don't want to wake up ten years from now and say, 'My God, who is this I've married?' So it scares me a little bit, but I think it's the right thing to do."

In the meantime, Oprah started collecting books on the topic of marriage soon after their engagement was announced. They included, Martha Stewart's *Wedding*, Eleanor Munro's *Wedding Readings* and a paperback, *Wedding Planner*.

"I am in no hurry to get married," she revealed to a reporter in early 1994. "I dislike this notion of a desperate woman who wants to get married . . . All the shows I've done on marriages give me more cause to examine it."

Meanwhile, Stedman told friends, "Whenever she's ready, I am."

Perhaps one reason that Oprah and Stedman aren't in any hurry to marry is because they already recognize the deep feelings of love they possess for one another. Regardless of whether or not they ever do become husband and wife, Oprah and Stedman's relationship has become ever closer since they started sharing a home together. In 1991 Stedman moved into Oprah's plush, six-bedroom condo overlooking Lake Michigan. Whenever possible, they also try to spend weekends together at her Indiana farm or at the 90-acre chalet Oprah purchased in the skiing town of Telluride, Colorado.

Stedman has also been instrumental in helping Oprah confront the pain she's carried for several years as a result of the sexual abuse she suffered as a young girl at the hands of different relatives. In the early nineties, Oprah revealed that not only was she abused by a cousin from her mother's side of the family, but also by her father's brother, Trent. In stark contrast to Stedman's willingness to help Oprah confront her pain, she experienced difficulty turning to her own family for similar support. Consequently, it affected Oprah's feelings toward them. "What makes me resentful is their unwillingness to accept my feelings," she offered. Acknowledging the phenomenal success she's experienced in the last several years, Oprah added, "They now want to pretend as though our past did not happen. I'm not the favorite daughter, favorite sister, as you can imagine." It particularly bothered Oprah that she and her father hadn't talked about her being sexually abused by his brother. As a young girl, Oprah tried to tell Vernon and his wife Zelma about what happened when she visited their home in Nashville from Milwaukee, but their own feelings of discomfort over the matter prompted them to ignore Oprah's allegations and she resolved not to bring it up with them again. In his defense, Vernon explained to *McCall's* magazine that he hadn't shared a private "twenty-minute conversation with Oprah in twenty years. There are people always around her."

Taking on the role of mediator, Stedman secretly boarded a plane to Nashville and met with Vernon for a very candid and intimate conversation. During the exchange, Stedman stressed the importance of Vernon's initiating a conversation with Oprah that would include talking about the sexual abuse she experienced as a child. Stedman's visit inspired Vernon to arrange a trip to Oprah's farm in Indiana. Finally, they talked as father and daughter about what happened. The conversation concluded with Vernon saying he was sorry.

Surprisingly, the loving support Stedman has shown Oprah prompted her to make an ironic observation. "I feel bad about this. I haven't been as nurturing and affectionate with him as I would have been had he treated me worse," she conceded to a reporter. "Throughout my life I have done the most incredible things for men who treated me like shit. For my first boyfriend I remember going into the kitchen and making an omelet. If it was a little lopsided, I threw it out and started over, to make sure it was perfect. But now I'm attracted to somebody who doesn't require that. Where I don't have to say, 'Look, look, I'm good—will you stay, please?' . . . I really do think I don't do enough for him."

Professionally, Oprah continued to grow by leaps and bounds in the early nineties. To accommodate her expanded workload serving as the chief executive officer of Harpo Productions, Oprah occasionally began taping two episodes a day of her talk-show four days a week, so that she could give bigger blocks of time to her other responsibilities. In an interview with *TV Guide*, Oprah admitted she noticed a difference and that eventually it could have an influence in determining how much longer she wanted to continue hosting. "I can't do these shows with the intensity I used to. I started out doing five shows a week, one a day. Compared to what we do now—sometimes shooting two shows a day, four days a week—that was a breeze. When I lose my passion for it, I'll quit. Of course, I know nobody believes me, because even my friends say, 'You're gonna give up that money? No!'"

As a result of becoming a world-famous celebrity, Oprah also noticed that her own feelings about interviewing well-known movie stars and TV-personalities had changed. "Interviewing celebrities used to scare me. I thought they were so different from what I was. I had them up on a pedestal ... But when I became a celebrity myself, I realized that celebrity is based upon other people's perceptions. It has absolutely nothing to do with who I am. I'm not the person people write about, and neither, I find, are the celebrities I talk to."

Besides continuing her daytime TV talk-show, Oprah also branched into prime-time television in 1992 with a series of specials titled "Behind the Scenes" that featured on-location interviews with such movie stars as Dustin Hoffman, Meryl Streep, Goldie Hawn, Jodie Foster and Richard Gere. "This is the première of the prime-time," she told a reporter shortly before the first installment aired. "Things are really just beginning for me. 'Behind the Scenes' could not have happened without the daytime 'Oprah Winfrey Show' as a foundation. Because we've done so well in daytime, the network trusts that we might also be able to do well at night."

Soon after, Oprah scored an even bigger coup when she persuaded an extremely shy Michael Jackson to be interviewed live on national television from his ranch, Neverland, in Santa, Ynez, for ninety minutes. It would be Jackson's first televised interview in fourteen years. "Michael Jackson has always been at the top of my list of people I am most interested in interviewing," Oprah said. "The excitement of this interview being live and unedited is certainly a special event for me and for all of Michael's fans."

Oprah looked forward to conducting the interview because it would provide Jackson with an opportunity to squelch the myriad rumours that had surfaced surrounding his reclusive lifestyle, including if he really bleached his skin, or slept in a glass-enclosed oxygen chamber. But she drew the line on questioning the talented singer about his sex life or preferences. "I don't think that's anybody's business," Oprah explained. "I wouldn't ask *anybody* that."

The highly anticipated special was broadcast live to sixty countries and seen by an estimated ninety million viewers. The day after the special aired on ABC-TV, the network proudly announced it was seen by fifty-six percent of the households tuned into television on that evening. It also ranked as the fourth-highest rated entertainment special, preceded only by the final episode of "MASH," the episode of "Dallas" that revealed who shot J.R. Ewing and *The Day After*, a 1983 TV-movie about the survivors of a nuclear Holocaust.

In addition to interviewing celebrities, a public-minded Oprah also hosted a prime-time documentary special titled, "Scared Silent: Exposing and Ending Child Abuse." It was the first non-news show to be simulcast on the CBS, NBC and PBS national network television stations on September 4, 1992 (it was also broadcast two days later on ABC-TV). The special featured both victims and perpetrators telling their stories. Oprah, who introduced each segment, also added her own story to the special when she greeted the TV-viewing audience by saying, "I'm Oprah Winfrey, and like millions of other Americans, I am a survivor of child abuse. I was only nine years old when I was raped by my nineteen-year-old cousin. He was the first of three family members to sexually molest me."

The unprecedented special was only one part of Oprah's

crusade to protect children from being sexually abused. In February 1991, Oprah was inspired to draft legislation that would form a national data bank of convicted child abusers after hearing about the tragic murder of Angelica Mena, a four-year-old Chicago-area girl who had been brutally molested, strangled and tossed into Lake Michigan by a convicted child molester who lived next door to her family's home. To increase the legislation's odds of passing through Congress, Oprah hired Jim Thompson, a former Illinois Governor, to help her draft the bill. Oprah's hope was that a national data bank of convicted child abusers would make it possible for child-care organizations to investigate the background of prospective employees. In November 1992, Oprah testified before the Senate Judiciary Committee. The bill made it through the committee with flying colors, but was eventually defeated in Congress when it was made part of a crime package that included "The Brady Bill," a controversial gun-control proposal that was feverishly opposed by the National Rifle Association. A determined Oprah, however, revised the bill and it was eventually signed into law by President Clinton in December 1993 with Oprah proudly standing by his side.

Oprah also found time to produce and star in a prime-time TV-movie for ABT-TV titled *There Are No Children Here*, based on a bestselling nonfiction book about a single mother who lives in a dangerous Chicago public housing project with her two pre-teen sons and her efforts to protect them from the brutality of the streets. The TV-movie scored impressive ratings and reminded viewers of Oprah's Oscar-nominated dramatic talents.

In March 1994, Oprah put to rest fierce speculation that she would break ties with syndicator King World Productions when she renegotiated her TV talk-show contract beyond 1995. The new deal succeeded in giving Oprah even more control over her program, as well as the potential to earn higher profits. King World persuaded Oprah to extend her contract by five years, but after 1996 she had the option to decide annually if she wanted to renew. Although the renegotiated contract was considered advantageous for King World because it gave the syndicator the exclusive right to distribute "The Oprah Winfrey Show" through the year 2000, Oprah was the one who actually landed herself a considerably better deal. During the first two years of the new deal, King World would continue to yield approximately 43 per cent of the show's profits, but in the third year, the terms revert to a distribution deal that leans more favorably in Oprah's corner, with King World enjoying only 25 per cent to 35 per cent of the profits and Oprah's company, Harpo Productions, getting the rest. With the new deal, Oprah also became one of King World's largest shareholders. In early 1994 she already controlled a million shares of the company, but her new contract made it possible for her to buy another 500,000 shares, plus options to buy an additional 250,000 shares a year each time she renews the show from 1997 through 2000.

Oprah also tops *Forbes* magazine's list of the wealthiest entertainers with a two-year total of $98 million. Taking into account the earnings she's made in nine years of broadcasting her talk-show, Oprah has made nearly a quarter of a billion dollars. She's also considered an "odds-on favorite" to make the prestigious Forbes 400 list by 1995.

By that same year Oprah is also hoping to produce feature films. She's already commissioned the first drafts of scripts for two movies, one based on Toni Morrison's Pulitzer Prize-winning novel, *Beloved*, which explores the difficulties a woman encounters after escaping slavery, and the second for Zora Neale Hurston's *Their Eyes Are Watching God*, a story that follows a woman's evolution through three marriages. Friends close to Oprah say she's planning to assume the lead role in *Beloved*, with filming tentatively scheduled to begin by the summer of 1995.

In early 1993, the publishing world was buzzing about

Oprah's autobiography, which was scheduled to be published in September 1993, by Knopf. Before a single word has been committed to paper by Oprah and her collaborator, journalist Joan Barthel, Knopf already had orders for 750,000 copies. An editor at a competing publishing house was confident Knopf could bring the order up to two million before the manuscript was even completed. Oprah's influence in selling books was already legendary to publishers. Soon after she devoted an hour of her show to the bestselling novel, *The Bridges of Madison County*, an additional 350,000 copies were shipped to bookstores. To tout her own highly anticipated book, Oprah appeared at the American Booksellers Association in late May in Miami and revealed that "this is going to be a book that really empowers people."

But two weeks later, on June 15, Oprah dropped a bombshell that sent the publishing world reeling. After serious and heart-wrenching soul-searching, Oprah decided against publishing her autobiography. Her public announcement included this statement, "I'm in the heart of the learning curve. I feel there are important discoveries yet to be made."

Naturally, several rumors quickly arose regarding the *real* reason Oprah nixed her book. One source said Oprah didn't think the book was good enough. Others who knew Oprah believed that she wasn't ready to make a full disclosure regarding the sexual abuse she suffered as a child. Yet another source implied that Stedman was unhappy with the book. "He didn't say anything was too explicit or shouldn't be said," Oprah insisted. "He said it wasn't powerful enough . . . I made the ultimate decision."

The weekend before Oprah made her unexpected announcement, she visited her Indiana farmhouse. She sought solitude in a nearby log cabin located in the grounds. On the porch was a swing that was identical to the one at the first house where she lived in Mississippi with her grandmother. While quietly rocking back and forth on the swing, with the summer breeze lightly touching her face, Oprah tearfully decided that the time wasn't right for her to publish an autobiography. "I prayed and cried, sitting on the swing," Oprah revealed. "I feel bad about disappointing people. I went back on my word." But in the bigger scheme of things, Oprah soon realized that she had reached a new stage in her own personal development. "I finally said, 'Congratulations. You have always done what other people expected of you, and now you've done something for yourself,'" she explained.

The process of writing her autobiography proved to be extremely beneficial to Oprah. Finally, she was able to understand why she over-ate. "Some women have convinced themselves that being overweight is genetic and that's who they are. I know my weight's about emotional problems," Oprah candidly admitted. On a separate occasion she added, "My biggest failure was in believing that the weight issue was just about weight. It's not. It's about not being able to say no. It's about not handling stress properly. It's about sexual abuse. It's about all the things that cause other people to become alcoholics and drug addicts."

Oprah quickly realized that understanding the problem was only half the battle. Determined to shed her unwanted pounds in a healthy way, Oprah hired a personal trainer, Bob Greene, in March 1993. During their first consultation he explained why Oprah's earlier, highly touted Optifast diet was doomed to failure. Although Oprah shed more than sixty pounds on the liquid diet, she also lost significant muscle tissue. Greene pointed out that, even at a 145 pounds, twenty-eight percent of her weight was still fat. "You're sort of like a calorie sponge," Green explained. "You're waiting for any calorie to come along so you can absorb it and turn it into fat." To help Oprah lose weight efficiently, Greene devised a twice-daily aerobic workout regime that would also assist in boosting her metabolism. Oprah rose every morning at 5:30 A.M. for a rigorous workout with Greene. Working in tandem with Greene, Oprah also set monthly fitness goals and various strategies for achieving them. In the beginning, she walked quickly on a treadmill, then she worked her way up to a slow jog. Within months, Oprah was running up to eight miles, spending forty-five minutes on the Stairmaster and successfully completing 350 sit-ups. She could also run a mile in under eight minutes. "People told me running would be fun," Oprah said. "When I first started, I said, 'What's fun about this?'" But after participating in the 13-mile San Diego Half Marathon in two hours and sixteen-minutes, Oprah exclaimed, "Today was a lot of fun!" She was also proud to discover that she had completed her run only an hour behind the first-place winner.

There was also a complete change in the meals Oprah ate. After failing at several different diets because they were so strict and unexciting. Oprah resolved that she wanted to still be able to *enjoy* the food she ate. To make that possible, Oprah hired a personal chef, Rosie Daley, who previously served in a similar position for the exclusive Cal-a-Vie Spa in San Diego, California. With Daley's help, Oprah was able to enjoy pizza and sweet-potato pie. The only difference was that Rosie kept Oprah's fat intake to twenty grams a day (the same amount that could be found in two tablespoons of mayonnaise).

By the fall of 1993, Oprah lost fifty pounds by eating three sensible meals a day and sticking to her twice-daily workouts. Oprah's new system included three significant factors that weren't a part of her earlier, failed crash-diets: proper nutrition, daily exercise and self-knowledge. As a result, Oprah gleefully discovered that not only were the pounds coming off, they were *staying* off.

Surprisingly, not everyone was happy about the new, improved body Oprah was busy designing for herself. One morning, while she was jogging along a road near her Indiana farm, a woman approached her and warned, "You better quit losing weight, because you're going to make the rest of us feel bad." But the self-knowledge Oprah was developing quickly gave her insight into the hidden subtext behind the woman's good-natured warning. "What she really meant was, 'Listen, if you start looking better than I do, I'm not going to like you anymore,'" Oprah keenly observed.

On November 16, 1993, Oprah dedicated yet another installment of her show to dieting. It was exactly five years and a day after she sported a pair of size 10 Calvin Klein jeans while pulling a wagonful of fat onto her stage. Once again, Oprah stood before her audience looking svelte. But this time she was eager to share the differences that had made her new weight-loss possible. She informed an awestruck audience that since March, when she tipped the scales at two-hundred and twenty-two pounds, she had run one thousand, four-hundred-and-fifty-two miles, hiked forty-three point seven miles and lost seventy-two pounds.

On January 29, 1994, Oprah celebrated her fortieth birthday. She marked the occasion with a lavish dinner-party at a posh, LA-area restaurant. The guests included network news anchorwoman Maria Shriver, film director Steven Spielberg and musician Quincy Jones. After the party, Oprah dismissed the fellows and retreated to the Bel-Air Hotel with her close female friends, where she enjoyed her first slumber party.

At forty, the fun was just beginning for Oprah.

Selected
Bibliography

Anderson, Chris. "Meet Oprah Winfrey." *Good Housekeeping* (August 1986).

_____."Oprah Winfrey Conquers 'The Tonight Show.'" *Chicago Tribune* (January 31, 1985).

_____. "Wingin' It With Channel 7's Oprah Winfrey." *The Chicago Tribune* (March 3, 1984).

Bailey, Greg. "Oprah Winfrey Debuts Monday." *The Nashville Banner* (September 6, 1986).

Ballard, Gary, "Oprah Winfrey." *Drama-Logue* (March 20, 1986).

Barthel, Joan. "Here Comes Oprah." *Ms.* (August 1986).

_____. "Oprah Winfrey Rides Whirlwind." *The Chicago Sun-Times* (February 24, 1985).

_____. "Talk Show Diva Named Oprah." *Channels* (January 1986).

_____. "When Nothing's Off Limits." *The Chicago Sun-Times* (July 2, 1984).

_____. "Winfrey's Dream Hits High Gear." *The Chicago Sun-Times* (May 22, 1984).

Brady, Mary Jo. "Director Says TV Needs Women." *The Nashville Banner* (March 24, 1975).

Carter, Bill. "Baltimore's First News Hours." *The Baltimore Sun* (August 13, 1976).

_____."Channel 2 Gets Oprah." *The Baltimore Sun* (August 2, 1985).

_____. "Oprah Winfrey: Still Talk of the Town." *The Baltimore Sun* (September 9, 1986).

_____. "Winfrey Show Goes On." *The Baltimore Sun* (August 19, 1986).

_____ "WJZ-TV Announces News Shake-Up." *The Baltimore Sun* (April 2, 1977).

Cedrone, Lou. "She's Very Natural." *The Baltimore Sun* (March 18, 1986).

Chunovic, Louis. "ABC Wants Oprah." *Hollywood Reporter* (February 27, 1987).

Class, Kelly. "Making a TV Star Into a Mogul." *Adweek* (January 20, 1987).

DePaulo, Lisa. "Oprah's Private Life." *TV Guide* (June 3, 1989).

225

DuBrow, Rick. "Winfrey vs.Mr. Sincerity." *The Los Angeles Times* (August 19, 1986).

———."with Cleage, Pearl. "Oprah: In Her Own Words." *Essence* (June 1989).

Edwards, Audrey, "Oprah Winfrey: Stealing the Show." *Essence* (October 1986).

Embry, Pat. "Oprah Winfrey Ready for Academy Award." *The Nashville Banner* (February 24, 1986).

———. "Oprah Winfrey's Father Says Her Success Is No Surprise." *The Nashville Banner* (January 20, 1986).

Feder, Robert. "Did Oprah Dazzle 'Em on 'Tonight Show'?" *The Chicago Sun-Times* (January 31, 1985).

———. "Oprah Winfrey Wows 'Em Across America." *The Chicago Sun-Times* (September 16, 1986).

Gillespie, Martha Ann. "Winfrey Takes All." *MS* (December, 1988).

Giuliano, Mike. "New 'Oprah Winfrey Show' Lookin' Like a Hit." *The Baltimore News American* (August 3, 1986).

Griffin, Nancy. "Us Inteview." *Us Magazine* (March 20, 1989).

Gross, Linden. "Wonder Woman." *Ladies Home Journal* (December 1988).

Grossberger, Lewis. "Can We Not Talk?" *Rolling Stone* (December 14, 1986).

Hammett, Corinne F. "Oprah Acts." *The Baltimore News American* (December 22, 1985).

Harmetz, Aljean. "Learning to Live With Runaway Fame." *The New York Times* (May 18, 1986).

———. "Problems of Filming *Native Son*." *The New York Times* (December 23, 1986).

Hunter, Stephen. "Just Oprah!" *The Baltimore Sun* (December 17, 1985).

Kearney, Jill. "Whoopi Goldberg: Color Her Anything." *American Film* (December 1985).

King, Patricia. "Move Over, Phil Donahue." *Family Circle* (October 21, 1986).

Littwin, Susan. "Oprah Opens Up." *TV Guide* (May 5, 1990).

Mansfield, Stephanie. "And Now, Heeere's Oprah!" *The Washington Post* (October 21, 1986).

Markey, Judy. "Brassy, Sassy Oprah Winfrey." *Cosmopolitan* (September 1986).

Matthews, Jack. "Three 'Color Purple' Actresses Talk About Its Impact." *The Los Angeles Times* (January 31, 1986).

Mayfield, Mark. "Oprah's Town Meeting." *USA Today* (February 10, 1987).

McKerrow, Steve. "Oprah's Show Is Like Donahue's." *The Baltimore Evening Sun* (September 9, 1986).

Mitchell, Deborah, "Oscar Shopping." *Us* (March 24, 1986).

Neisser, Judith. "Oprah Winfrey Putting Some Snap Into TV Talk Shows." *United* (December 1986).

Nelson, Jill. "The Man Who Saved Oprah Winfrey." *The Washington Post* (December 14, 1986).

Nelson, Jim, Sternig, Barbara. "Talk Show Star's Wild and Wicked Childhood." *National Enquirer* (March 20, 1990).

Noel, Pamela, "Lights! Camera! Oprah!" *Ebony* (April 1985).

Novit, Mel. "Talk of Chicago Is a Hit in *Purple*." *USA Today* (December 26, 1985).

Peterson, Karen S. "Toast of Chicago TV Goes National" and "Oprah Opens Up Her Own National Talk Show." *USA Today* (September 1986).

Pollen, Michael. "Jackpot!" *Channels* (June 1986).

Rautbord, Sugar. "Oprah." *Interview* (March 1986).

Richman, Alan. "Oprah." *People* (January 12, 1987).

Robertson, Nan. "Actresses' Varied Roads to *The Color Purple*." *The New York times* (February 13, 1986).

Rosenberg, Howard. "Winfrey Zeroing in on Donahue." *The Los Angeles Times* (September 12, 1986).

Roush, Matt. "Her Empire Grows with ABC Series." *USA Today* (May 5, 1990).

Sanders, Richard. "To the Top." *People* (December 16, 1985).

Sanders, Steve. "More than just Talk." *Hollywood Reporter.* (December 2, 1988).

Scott, Walter. "Personality Parade." *Parade Magazine* (May 6, 1990).

Shahoda, Susan. "Oprah Buys Chicago Film & Television Complex." *Backstage* (September 30, 1988).

_____."Oprah Sheds 67 Pounds For Herself, Not For Love." *Jet* (December 19, 1988).

Sherman, Eric. "Oprah Speaks From The Heart." *Ladies Home Journal* (May 1990).

Smith, R.C. "She Once Smashed Her Apartment to Make a Point." *TV Guide* (August 30, 1986).

Tassie, Nina. "Off-Camera With Richard and Oprah." *Messenger* (April 14, 1982).

Taubeneck, Anne. "TV Woman Who Is Not Afraid to Eat." *The Chicago Sun-Times* (April 23, 1984).

Tornabene, Lyn. "Here's Oprah!" *Woman's Day* (October 1, 1986).

Warren, Elaine. "Women of Brewster Place." *TV Guide* (March 18, 1989)

Waters, Harry F. "Chicago's Grand New Oprah." *Newsweek* (December 31, 1984).

Warren, Elaine. "Women of Brewster Place". *TV Guide* (March 18, 1989).

Whitaker, Charles. "TV's Most Talented TV Talk-Show Host." *Ebony* (March 1987).

Young, Luther. "*Color Purple's* Star Gets Baltimore's Red Carpet Treatment." *The Baltimore Sun* (February 21, 1986).

_____. "Oprah in the Soaps." *The Baltimore Sun* (February 28, 1983).

_____. "She's Found Success Just by Being Herself." *The Baltimore Sun* (January 27, 1985).

Zaslow, Jeffrey. "Morning Star." *Savvy* (September 1986).

_____."Oprah Goes National." *The Wall Street Journal* (March 7, 1986).

Zehme, Bill. "It Came From Chicago." *Spy* (December 1986).

Zogline, Richard. "People Sense the Realness." *Time* (September 15, 1986).

CHER

Her Life and Wild Times

Lawrence J. Quirk

As a teenager Cherilyn Sarkisian had a large nose, crooked teeth, poor posture and bad skin. She couldn't sing very well either, and at the start of her career was written off as a no-talent joke. Yet of all the stars in the Hollywood galaxy, few have undergone such a dramatic transformation, or have glittered as brightly, as controversially, and for as long as Cher. Now, in this revealing biography, the full, sensational story is told.

From her tempestuous relationship with her mother to the shocking controversy surrounding her own daughter; from her repressive years with the Svengali-like Sonny Bono to a string of highly-publicised affairs with Hollywood's hottest young male stars; from the inauspicious start of her career to her phenomenal success in both the movie and recording industries, Lawrence Quirk shatters the myths, explores the legends and takes a very private look at the life of this fascinating superstar.

DEPARDIEU
A BIOGRAPHY

Marianne Gray

'A highly enjoyable read ... a fascinating insight into the
career and character of possibly the best screen actor of
our time'
BARRY NORMAN

Unorthodox sex symbol, Europe's most controversial and
acclaimed actor, Hollywood's hottest new property, the
single-handed saviour of the French cinema and veteran
of over seventy films, Gérard Depardieu is the latest
international superstar.

Yet the real Gérard Depardieu is something of an
enigma. Now, in this revealing biography – the first to
appear in English – Marianne Gray charts his life from
the adolescent forays into petty crime in the unalluring
French town of Châteauroux to the present jet-set
existence, giving us a true portrait of the complex man
behind the myths. Fully documenting the film career that
exploded onto the international scene with *Jean de Florette*,
Manon des Sources, his Oscar-nominated performance in
Cyrano de Bergerac and *Green Card* which won him a Golden
Globe, she also covers his work in the theatre, work that
he takes as seriously as his much-publicised devotion to
good food and fine wine. And delving into his private life,
the author reveals his attitude to his marriage, his friends
and family – and the truth behind the rape scandal that
rocked the world's tabloid press.

'Full of fascinating anecdotes and rare stills – highly
recommended'
Screen International

PFEIFFER

Beyond the Age of Innocence

Douglas Thompson

From checkout girl to Catwoman, *naïveté* and innocence to Scorsese and *The Age of Innocence*, Michelle Pfeiffer has come a long way. Now one of the most powerful women in Hollywood, commanding multi-million dollar fees, combining looks and talent and acting opposite many of the screen's top stars, Michelle Pfeiffer seems to have it all.

In this, the first full-length biography of Pfeiffer, acclaimed Hollywood-watcher Douglas Thompson unveils the mysteries behind her transformation from high school beauty to Hollywood player. The wild early years; the brainwashing by a bizarre cult; the rocky romances with, among others, John Malkovich and Michael Keaton; the love of acting and the road to fame – Thompson has the inside story and makes full use of extensive interviews with Pfeiffer herself, her family, friends and colleagues to present a fascinating and intimate portrait of one of the industry's hottest stars.

GODDESS: THE SECRET LIVES OF MARILYN MONROE

Anthony Summers

The definitive investigation of Marilyn Monroe's mysterious death, meticulously researched and fully documented . . . the ultimate book on the ultimate sex symbol. GODDESS is the result of more than two years' investigation. Anthony Summers has drawn on an unsurpassed mine of evidence to reveal the truth about many of the previously unanswered questions of Marilyn's life and death. He reveals the truth about Marilyn's frustrated love life; the complicated relationship with the intensely jealous Joe DiMaggio; the tragic failure of her marriage to Arthur Miller; her abortions and miscarriages; her private fantasies and fears; first-hand testimony about her close relationship with the Kennedys; Mafia conspiracies and Sinatra's role.

GODDESS is the ultimate probe into the life of the woman who, long after her death, continues to mesmerize the world.

A TIME TO SPEAK

Anthony Quayle

'A remarkable book by a remarkable man ...
extraordinarily exciting reading'
Sunday Telegraph

The great, unacknowledged giant of the postwar British
classical theatre, Anthony Quale was also an
internationally respected actor and director, the force
behind the present Royal Shakespeare Company, and
perhaps the last of the great actor-managers who have
done so much to foster the traditions of contemporary
theatre. To the cinema-going public, too, films such as
The Guns of Navarone, *Ice Cold in Alex* and *Lawrence of
Arabia* made his name and distinctive features familiar
throughout the world.

He was also, as this much-acclaimed autobiography
reveals, a highly accomplished writer. A Lancashire
childhood that was often solitary and far from happy; a
remarkable love story; wartime adventures, politicians and
heroes; brilliant vignettes of an actor's life – all come
vividly alive in these pages. So too do the 'greats' of the
British theatre: John Gielgud, Lawrence Olivier, Ralph
Richardson, Peggy Ashcroft, Alec Guinness, Edith Evans
and many more.

'Utterly unlike any other actor's autobiography you are
likely to come across. It is elegantly written in simple
muscular English as down-to earth, resonant and honest
as the man himself, and shot through, page by page, with
an unforced sense of love for England and her language'
Sunday Telegraph